can be a sticky situation.

According to Bill Butterworth, family life is very much like peanut butter. At different times, it can be smooth or crunchy. But most importantly, like peanut butter on two slices of bread (or anything else it touches), families should stick together. In *Peanut Butter Families Stick Together*, Bill Butterworth offers a look at domestic living that will keep you in stitches as you learn that problems *do* have a purpose. He shows that to be committed to your family means to be committed to the *process* of raising a family—and accepting the struggles, tensions, and confusion as part of this process. By offering a humorous contrast between realism and idealism, he shows you that you're not alone in your struggles. You'll learn to laugh at what you see of yourself in these rib-tickling reflections on family life in the "real world." Once you've discovered the therapy of laughter, you'll find practical encouragement for the daily challenges of parenthood.

PEANUT BUTTER FAMILIES STICK TOGETHER

BILL BUTTERWORTH

Power Books

Fleming H. Revell Company
Old Tappan, New Jersey

Library of Congress Cataloging in Publication Data

Butterworth, Bill.
    Peanut butter families stick together.

    "Power books."
    1. Family—Anecdotes, facetiae, satire, etc.
I. Title.
PN6231.F3B87   1985   814'.54   84-22319
ISBN 0-8007-5181-7

To Rhonda, my wife:
Like peanut butter sticketh
to the roof of the mouth,
So does a good wife to her husband.
Thank you for sticking with me.
I love you.

Contents

Introduction

If you knew the man who wrote this book as well as I know him ... you'd buy it. No questions asked, no hesitation.

Bill Butterworth may not be as well-known as Vince Lombardi or Tom Landry or John Wooden, but he's no less a winner. And on top of all that, he's a lot more fun! He is a creative thinker, a perceptive observer of life, a devoted husband of one wife, and the father of four blondes—all 100 percent busy. Which qualifies him to write ... and does he write! There may come the day when Butterworth will give Bombeck a run for her money. As a staff member of my radio ministry, Bill is already becoming known, thanks to his regular contributions to the printed study guides we publish at Insight for Living.

I first met Bill under a big bridge in south Florida. The tide was rising and his inner tube had sprung a leak, but that smile of his remained intact. Then and there I realized the man had an admirable sense of humor and an adventurous streak—my kinda guy.

No, I'm kidding. It just *looked* like he was under a bridge. With wall-to-wall kids, dirty dishes, pots, and pans strewn across the tiny kitchen, and a dizzy, mile-a-minute schedule to keep, it was easy to identify with the Butterworth family. I realized back then—it was quite a few years ago—that if the man lived through that, he owed it to the public to write about it.

Here's Bill's first attempt at letting it all hang out . . . and it's hilarious. But, better than that, it is real stuff, life as you and I know it. Only we just can't say it as well as this man can. Trust me, we will see a lot more of Bill Butterworth in print, especially if you and thousands like you buy this first one. If not, it'll make a great collector's item!

No chance. This thing is as tasty as peanut butter and twice as addictive. Just take a peek and try to stop with one page—I dare you!

Chuck Swindoll

Cast of
Characters

Joy

Age: Six
Occupation: *Only daughter, full-time firstborn.*
A wonderful blend of lovely little girl and tough little tomboy. An expert at wrapping Dad around her little finger.

Jesse

Age: Five
Occupation: *Self-appointed answer man.*
The brain in the family. Sometimes talks like an adult, but carries mature thoughts around in a child's body.

Jeffrey

Age: Questionable
Occupation: *Trying to decide whether he's two or three. He walks around sucking his thumb, carrying a blanket, and occasionally delivering one-liners that blow us all away.*

Cast of Characters

John   Age: Infant
Occupation: *Eats, sleeps, wets.*
Eats everything in sight, whether edible or not. Sleeps only at inappropriate times, never when we want him to. Wets whenever we're ready to go somewhere.

Rhonda   Age: In her own words, "It's really not important."
Occupation: *As a wife, she loves her husband and endures his off-the-wall attitudes toward life. As a mother, she's loving, flexible, creative, and fun to be around. She's a perfect "straight woman" for my jokes and an expert at facial expressions.*

Bill   Age: Subtract Tom Selleck's age from Wimpy's age.
Occupation: *Husband, father, breadwinner, lover of all the above characters.*
Sometimes talks like a child, but carries childlike thoughts around in an adult's body.

PEANUT BUTTER FAMILIES STICK TOGETHER

Peanut Butter Families Stick Together

The Peanut Butter Family ... is there one in your house?

At our house peanut butter serves a variety of uses besides the obvious use of being eaten. My kids enjoy peanut butter on their clothes, in their hair, around their ankles, and, of course, on their hands. Since it's on their hands, it allows them to share the wealth with Mom and Dad. Yes, we often have peanut butter pots and pans, peanut butter dress shirts, peanut butter pliers, and peanut butter appliances. Naturally, this is usually discovered while sitting at a peanut butter table in a peanut butter chair.

Peanut butter is not only a staple of life, it's also responsible for a great deal of family cohesiveness.

Does this sound like your place? Did you think yours was the only family to wrestle with the peanut butter problem? Did you think you were the only mom whose kitchen resembled a peanut butter jar? Or did you think you were the only dad going to work with peanut butter on his clothes?

Unless I miss my guess, a lot of us parents are walking around a little bit sticky. Peanut butter will do that to you—and that's just fine.

You see, life is like peanut butter; it can be smooth, or it can be crunchy. But, for most of us, it's crunchy a lot more of the time. The occasional smooth easiness of life is a welcome relief to those crunchy, crazy, confusing days.

The Peanut Butter Family symbolizes the realistic family process that goes on in homes everywhere. You're not alone, my friends. The more we can learn to laugh at all this, the better off we'll be.

That's why I wrote this book. But let me spell it out in greater detail.

One purpose of this book is to contrast idealism with realism.

There are a ton of success-oriented books out there on the topic of family living; and don't get me wrong, I want a successful family as much as the next chump. It's just that . . . I resemble Dagwood Bumstead a lot more than I resemble Superman.

So I'm suggesting "realistic success," instead of "idealistic success." The difference is huge.

Idealism tells you that you are free from problems because you're a Christian. Not so. Scripture says that you become a Christian through trusting Christ as Savior by faith. But your faith will be tested in order to produce

Peanut Butter
Families
Stick Together

patience which ultimately matures you into further Christlikeness.

Realism tells you that your life is far from problem free; but the problems have purpose. They teach us valuable lessons. The best attitude to have is one of teachability.

Idealism is best represented by our Sunday morning best. It is free from wrinkles, sitting quietly in a pew, untouched by humanity.

Realism is Saturday evening after a hard day of work and play—grass-stained knees from sliding into third base, muddy fingers from playing with trucks in the petunias, sawdust hair from buzz sawing some plywood, no makeup, dirty diapers, grape jelly around the left earlobe, unholy holey T-shirts, a ball game on television, newspapers spread all over the living room, bowls of popcorn, empty cans of Pepsi, fatigue, attitude problems, whiny kids, grumpy parents, exhaustion.

I can't explain why, but in a typical week there are more "Saturday evenings" than "Sunday mornings."

Idealism teaches us perfect family living based on the Bible.

Realism tells us that the Bible presents principles for our encouragement—but no promises of perfection.

Perfection is reserved for Heaven. I can't expect perfect family living when the family is made up of imperfect people. And where there is imperfection, there is tension. There is calamity, chaos, confusion, and sometimes comedy.

We all live with a series of tensions, constantly in demand of resolve and balance. That's where the realistic approach comes in. The Bible is full of guidelines to aid in bringing the resolve.

It doesn't erase tension, it eases it.

So plug into reality, my friends. Idealistic success is as easy to catch as the wind. Realistic success is as easy to catch as a cold.

If we accept life realistically, we must understand this next concept:

To commit yourself to your family is to commit yourself to the *process* that goes with it.

Family life is lived daily in most homes. In order to live through it, we must adjust our thinking. We tend to dwell on products, results, and happy endings. In doing so, we neglect the process.

As a Christian husband and father, I have committed myself to God and my family. Ideally, that should make everything fine, but in reality it's just the beginning of the craziness.

Every day is a new learning experience, not just for the kids, but for Mom and Dad as well. So Jesse wants to learn how to tie his shoes. I can be angry, abrasive, demanding, stubborn, unbending, and merciless on the little guy in order to achieve the result—a kid who can tie his shoes.

Or, I can cool my jets and help him work through the process ... day after day ... month after month, if necessary.

The kids inspire me by tolerating my plodding through the process. They know I make mistakes. I can't rely on years of experience. I'm new at most of this stuff.

But they are willing to help me work through the process.

Why can't I extend the same courtesy to them?

I know more about my kids today than I did yesterday. My education is a process of pain and pleasure. Both make me stronger.

It's sad to think about all the parents who miss the

process. It happens all the time. Some kids even turn out just fine; but a valuable element is missing.

For if I miss the process, I miss part of the core of the family unit. I can superficially enjoy the shell, but there is so much more.

This book was also written to encourage fellow moms and dads. I hope this message comes through to you:

Mom and Dad, you are not alone in your struggles.

When you hang around idealistic people, it's easy to believe that everybody has it all together while you sit in frenzied frustration.

That's a myth.

Listen, fellow parents, we all have the crazy days of life. You've been there.

We all have depressed appliances. We all have Saturdays. We all struggle to sit like saints in church. We all shop for groceries, go to pediatricians, fight for parking spots, tolerate car pools, and endure Back-to-School Nights.

Fight the feeling of isolation.

It's so easy to block out everyone. Sitting in an alienated environment is dangerous to your health.

Start some new friendships. How about a group of parents who meet to support and encourage one another toward realistic success?

Idealism isolates. Realism rallies.

Don't be embarrassed. You are not alone. There's strength in numbers.

Well, there is one more reason behind the words in this book. In a sense, this may have been the biggest motivation in my mind:

We must learn to laugh at ourselves.

I don't know if anyone has ever told you this, but I will: Some of the stuff you do as a family is funny.

Come on, now. You know I'm right.

You're smiling right now, because your brain is flooding with memories that make you laugh. Sure, they may not have been funny at the time, but now they border on hysterical.

Here's how I look at it. Every day we are faced with a series of family events. Our responses go in one of two possible directions:

A. One way to respond is with anger, frustration, tension, and anxiety.

B. The other response is a big, old belly laugh.

Response A produces ulcers. Response B makes memories.

Make a commitment with me. Let's commit that in the days ahead, we will learn to laugh more.

So be encouraged, my friends, the Peanut Butter Family exists today—everywhere! You must decide how you will respond to life's looney tunes.

The choice is yours. You can become an ulcerated idealist or a smiling realist.

One becomes more and more frustrated.

The other has more and more fun.

One of the "funnest" fathers I know is Chuck Swindoll. I've worked for him for the past few years, and if there's one lesson I've learned from him it can best be summarized in this little maxim: Take God seriously . . . but don't take yourself so seriously.

Our Christian bookstores are filled with books on taking God seriously—and that is good. But, where are the books that help us with the other side?

When will Christians be allowed to discover the therapy of laughter? We've been sneaking smiles for years. It's time to come out of the closet. Life is funny—the Christian life has its chuckles as well.

So let's give cause for believers to belly laugh. This book is for every mom or dad who's ever exclaimed, "It's been one of those days!"

Christianity needs this book like peanut butter needs jelly.

The Peanut Butter Families of the world must stick together!

2

Depression
Among Appliances

We all know the great American dream ... a house of our own. You apartment dwellers know the longing, don't you? No more wasted rent payments, I'll build equity through my valuable asset. No more landlords, I'll be the king of my own domain. No more banging neighbors above, below, or side to side; I'll play my stereo as loud as I want. No more staring at the fake grass on the welcome mat, I'll have a lawn ... a real live lawn for the kids to play on.

If you're a homeowner already, you'll remember the longing: white picket fences, neighborhoods filled with pie-baking neighbors, friendly pets, Cub Scouts, Brownies, wood-paneled station wagons parked in the driveways with the morning paper resting peacefully by the front porch swing.

Eleven years in a small apartment sure had the Butterworth family hungering for a house. Finally, the dream came true. A change in jobs caused a move from a Florida apartment to a California home.

Moving day was in late June, and the weather was made to order by the local chamber of commerce. Sure, the house was a little small, a little old, a little bland—but hey, this is the American dream. It's gonna be perfect!

We had an answer for everything:

Not enough bedrooms	*— The kids will learn the real meaning of fellowship.*
Antiquated kitchen	*— We'll eat out a lot.*
One bathroom for six people	*— Several of the kids are still bedwetters.*
Backyard looks like a jungle	*— Great "foreign missionary experience" for the kids.*
No fireplace	*— We'll systematically burn down parts of the backyard jungle.*
We have too much furniture and stuff	*— But we have a garage.*
We have a car	*— But we have a street.*
The garage isn't attached to the house	*— We won't sort through the stuff unless fully dressed.*

The interest rate is	*— It's great for tax de-*
too high	*duction purposes.*
The house payment	*— We can all afford*
is so big	*to skip some meals.*

We had totally convinced ourselves that this was our dream house. We eagerly wrote our apartment-dwelling friends back in Florida, telling them all about what they were missing. July was a delight. We were on a honeymoon with our house. All was tidy, efficient, well-ordered, running properly, a real pleasure palace.

Then it happened.

The most horrendous heat wave we had ever experienced. Each day seemed to press closer and closer to 170 degrees. Evenings it cooled down to 135. It was a killer. We asked our neighbors about this incredible natural phenomenon. What was the cause of this torturous temperature, this morbid melt, this frenzied fry, this brutal boil? Their answer was simple and to the point:

"It's August," they said.

"But we're from Florida, the home of humidity. We've never had it like this!" we replied.

"Was your apartment in Florida air-conditioned?"

"Yes."

"Is your house air-conditioned?"

"No."

"Think it through, Friend!"

We quickly turned to the classified section of the newspaper. Before all the ink melted onto our hands, we saw a used room air conditioner available at a reasonable price.

"I'll go buy it for you," I nobly stated. "My family is not going to drown in a sea of sweat, a puddle of perspiration, a lake of—"

"Just go get the air conditioner," Rhonda interrupted, obviously weak from heat and listening to me.

Once at the home of the air conditioner, I was met by its owner. "This is a great investment," he began, all the while puffing on his cigar. "We just air-conditioned our whole house. I finally got smart."

I reluctantly bought his room air conditioner. Two things bothered me:

1. When people tell me I'm making a great investment, I'm not.

2. He wasn't sweating.

I brought home our new (previously owned) room air conditioner amidst the cheers of my family. We decided the best place to put it was in the combination living room, dining room, family room, den, craft center, sewing room, study, play area. We did most of our perspiring in that one room.

By the time I got it installed the clock read 10:00 P.M. Of course, it was a lot cooler in the evening, but we wanted the exhilaration of seeing our breath.

We hit the ON button and huddled around the eight-inch vent. It was Minnesota all over again.

After we were all sufficiently frozen, we went to our bedrooms to thaw.

As I left for work the next morning, I possessed that special warm feeling a man gets by making the sacrifices necessary for his family's contentment.

That feeling is often referred to as being in debt.

Throughout the day as I sat in my air-conditioned office, I would think, *My family is home in their nice cool house. It is good to give thanks to the Lord.* Air conditioning is a prerequisite for true spirituality.

Rhonda called early that afternoon. I picked up the phone and said, "How's it going, my little Arctic circle?"

"I just thought you'd like to know," replied Rhonda, totally ignoring my Arctic circle remark, "that I'm sitting here in the living room watching all our candles melt."

"Have you used the air conditioner?"

"Yes, but it has a little problem."

"What's that?"

"It keeps blowing the circuits."

I sadly looked at the picture of my family on my desk. They all looked wet.

"I called the electric company," Rhonda continued. "They say it's a power surge. Too many people using too much electricity during the peak afternoon hours."

"So I spent all that money on an air conditioner that we can't use," I mumbled dejectedly.

"We can use it at night," was the weak reply of a melting mother.

After I hung up the phone, I went next door to see my boss. Ed was always encouraging. "This is so discouraging," I began. "What else could possibly go wrong?" Before Ed could even respond, the secretary came through on the intercom, "Bill, your wife's on line three."

Back in my office I picked up the phone. I could hear a horrendous sound even before I got the phone to my ear.

"Rhonda, is that you? Is everything all right?"

"HONKA, CHONKA, HONKA, CHONKA, HONKA, CHONKA."

"Rhonda, what is that terrible noise?"

"HONKA, CHONKA (It's) HONKA, CHONKA (the) HONKA, CHONKA (washing machine) HONKA, CHONKA."

"Are you in the laundry room?"

"(No, I'm) HONKA, CHONKA (in the) HONKA, CHONKA (living room)."

"Why is the sound so loud if you're in the living room?"

"HONKA, CHONKA (Because) HONKA, CHONKA (the washing machine is) HONKA, CHONKA (moving!)."

"IT'S MOVING?!?"

"(Yes) HONKA, CHONKA (it's heading toward) HONKA, CHONKA (Jeffrey!)."

That threw me for a real curve. After all, here was our chance to totally cleanse a two-year-old. I quickly regained my senses.

"Can you get to the socket to unplug it?"

"(I will) HONKA (pretty soon) CHONKA (it's almost) HONKA (out the front door) CHONKA!"

"Is anything wrong?" It was Ed, popping his head in the door.

"It's our washing machine," I replied. "It's tired of being fed only dirty clothes with junk in the pockets."

"So what's it doing?"

"It's refusing to work! It's on strike! It's in my front yard picketing this very moment!"

"That's too bad, man," Ed consoled.

"First the air conditioner, now the washing machine. Ed, I want to confess to you, I once used company stamps to send some personal mail."

"Bill, it's Rhonda again on line one."

"Rhonda, is it more bad news?"

"I'm afraid so."

"Then wait one second, Babe." I covered the mouthpiece of the phone and looked over at Ed. "It's more bad news ... so listen, Ed. ... Okay ... I'll admit ... it wasn't only stamps, I used company stationery too ... but I'll replace it all ... please forgive me ... beseech God on my behalf to remove His chastening rod ... I'll never steal again ... I'll start going to church on Sunday nights again ... I'll take up jogging ...."

"Relax, Bill, you're forgiven," Ed replied soothingly.

"Okay, Rhonda, what's the problem?" I asked nervously.

"The boys are watching TV," she calmly replied.

"So?"

"There's no picture ... only sound ... on all channels."

"That sounds bad," I moaned.

"Yes, the boys have had the TV on about thirty minutes. Any time now, they're going to notice that there's no picture. Any suggestions?"

"Ask them if they want to ride around the block in a washing machine."

I thought of all the guys I know who cheat on their taxes, and speed in their cars, and overeat, and don't use grass catchers. All of 'em were sitting in air-conditioned luxury. Meanwhile my godly family was sitting in the lake of fire, listening to TV, and chasing a washing machine.

"I wonder if Billy Graham has appliance problems?" I mused.

So as I drove home from work that evening, I had mixed feelings about it being Friday. *Well, at least I'll be with my family ... perhaps I can be more of an encouragement by being with them.* I thought to myself. Yet another voice inside was saying, *Work tomorrow, you chump! If not, you'll be the biggest basket case around and you'll drive your family crazy with your groaning!* To paraphrase the Apostle Paul: "The little voice I should listen to, I don't, and the little voice I shouldn't listen to, I do."

I stayed home Saturday.

Depression
Among Appliances

Our strategy could have taken one of two directions for this particular Saturday: (1) Dig in and get all this mess cleaned up, or (2) leave the house for the day and hope that if you ignore all the problems, they'll heal themselves. What's the real Christian thing to do?

We had a lovely time at the park.

Pools, picnics, and play sure helped pass the time. The house was the furthest thing from our minds as we simply enjoyed one another. Nonetheless, we eventually had to return. By mid-afternoon we had run out of diapers, food, and stuff to do. So at 4:00 P.M. we once again entered the melting pot with the unattached garage.

Our house looked like a stick of butter left out overnight.

We threw together some dinner from the miscellaneous items in the refrigerator. It wasn't till we had finished eating that we made the discovery that capped off our day—the refrigerator wasn't working.

The result was food poisoning—too morbid to describe on the printed page.

Since I was up all night, I had plenty of time to think. I guess I was guilty of believing a myth. I thought moving our family from an apartment to a house was the answer to all our worries and cares.

Maybe you've realized the same thing I did. It's futile to put your trust in things. They'll never live up to your expectations. Very few of us are realistic enough to plan on broken air conditioners, roaming washing machines, pictureless televisions, and warm refrigerators.

So learn from my mistake, okay?

Be careful where you put your trust or you, too, could end up suffering depression among appliances.

Saturday:
The Day of Rest

What's your Saturday like?

I like to think of it as my day of rest. (I'll explain in a later chapter why Sunday is far from restful!)

If you're like me, you think of Saturdays as a time for the hardworking man to kick back and enjoy a lazy day around the house. You know, sleep in late, don't shave, browse through the newspaper, nap in front of the tube, snack, rest up for the busy week ahead. It's even godly! Genesis 2 tells us God rested on the seventh day.

If resting on Saturday is godly, boy, am I a heathen!

Here's what Saturdays are usually like at our house: As I lay all snuggled in bed I heard the faint "click" of the alarm on the one day each week it's not set. I smiled to myself as I rolled over to perfect the science of sleeping in. While I was rolling over, my eyes sleepily focused on our two-year-old.

He was standing on the night table, getting ready to dive onto my face.

"Morning, Daddy," he yelled as he jumped. "Catch!"

I caught him in time to avoid surgery on either of us. He got a nose bleed; I got a headache, jammed thumb, and dizzy spells . . . but no surgery.

I got out of bed.

I looked at my alarm clock and it profanely informed me that "sleeping in" consisted of 2.6 minutes of extra sleep. *This has to be a terrorist plot,* I thought to myself as I splashed water on my face. Looking into the mirror, I observed that my two-year-old had left a footprint on my forehead.

I shuffled into the living room to discover that *all* the kids were already up watching Saturday morning cartoons. "You shouldn't watch that stuff," I mumbled. "You'll grow up to be a menace to society."

"Look at that, Dad!" yelled Jesse. "Brent Bent just turned into Styrofoam Man!"

"Hurray, hurray!" cheered Joy. "Now he'll be able to fight against the evil and sinister Asbestos Head!"

"Asbestos is stronger than styrofoam," I muttered, still half-asleep.

"Uh-uh, Dad, watch um!"

Sure enough Styrofoam Man turned Asbestos Head into something called Devious Dust.

By this time Rhonda came in and so I asked her, "Whatever happened to the real super heroes? Batman and Superman and those guys?"

"Their ratings were slipping. All they could do was fly and use superhuman strength. It was boring to the kids.

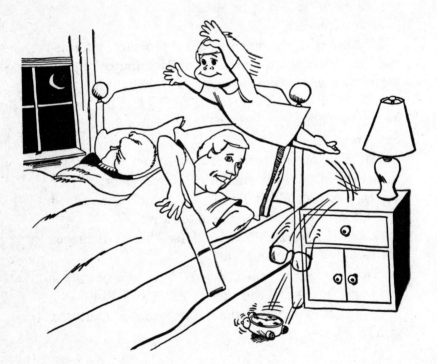

Saturday:
The Day of Rest

The networks came up with more versatile heroes like Styrofoam Man and his sidekick, Wax Boy."

I was immediately depressed. Really, how can you build a Saturday morning around a super hero named Wax Boy? "Come on, kids, you don't want to watch that stuff," I said.

"Well whatta ya wanna do today, Dad?" they asked.

"How about kicking back, browsing through the paper, snacking, napping, and generally resting up?"

They looked at me as if I had just threatened to melt Wax Boy.

"Well we can't hang around here watching this junk," I complained.

"Take it easy, Dad, it's almost over," comforted Joy. "You'll probably like the next show better. It's 'Rippo, the Nuclear Cow.' "

I was just about to spew forth, when Rhonda interjected, "How about going out to breakfast and then to a park!"

All the kids cheered. I prayed in silence to God.

You have to understand, going out to eat with the family is like Moses transporting the children of Israel out of Egypt. Moving the multitudes is no easy task.

I was tempted to dress in scuba gear, knowing that every time we eat out God makes us lie down in still water, juices, and milk. But instead, I just slipped into an old shirt and jeans that I would probably never be able to wear again. Just in case, I threw a snorkel in the car.

Restaurants never have the right size booth ready for us. As we strolled in I got set for my favorite pastime. Sure enough as the hostess watched the six of us walk in, I could see her counting us in her mind. Nevertheless, she delivered her classic line:

"How many?"

"Two adults and four children," responded Rhonda helpfully.

"That's six," I added, unable to resist conversation with the human computer.

"It will be just a few minutes while we set up your table."

Parties of two, three, four, and five came in and sat right down while we stood over in a corner waiting. "I hope they're still serving breakfast by the time we're seated," I griped.

We could see, at the very back of the restaurant, the construction crew responsible for setting up our table: two busboys, a waitress, one of the cooks, and the men from the surrounding three booths strenuously worked to create a booth with two seats for adults, two booster chairs, a high chair, and an infant seat/car seat combination that resembled a Volvo.

"Your table is ready," whispered the hostess wearily. We noticed a sudden hush fall over the restaurant as our troops marched in. Suddenly everyone began to gulp their food and demand their checks. We could only conclude that they had been in a restaurant with us before.

As the waitress distributed the menus, I started to think of the main reasons I enjoy this dining establishment:

1. It's cheap.
2. They serve coffee by the bowl.

Yet it's not without flaw. They have those ridiculous children's menus that can be reassembled into scale models of Disneyland. Joy had the fairy princess menu, Jesse had the rugged pioneer man menu, Jeffrey had the space traveler menu, and John's menu had already been eaten, thank you.

"Put my menu together first, Daddy!" they all cried in unison.

"Wait a minute, wait a minute," I protested. "You know I can't do anything like that till I've had my bowl of coffee. Just look at it for a while and decide what you want to eat."

I overheard Joy advising Jesse. "Pick this one, Jesse," she whispered. "It has the biggest number after it, so that means Daddy will yell 'cause it's 'spensive!"

"I heard that," I interrupted. "You will all get the usual."

"Dry cereal again?"

"That's right ... milk only if you're good children."

"What a rip-off," howled Jeffrey.

"That's enough of that, young man. Please play quietly with the toys you brought with you."

I'm unceasingly amazed at what kids can jam into their pockets. As they unloaded their treasures onto the table I just looked at Rhonda and sighed. "They have more stuff in their pockets than they have in their whole toy box!"

When the toys come out, so do the spills. There was liquid everywhere. "Man," I moaned. "I could swim back to the car."

I think we should declare Saturday morning breakfast an Olympic water sport.

"Are you ready to order?" Our waitress smiled like she lived in a Sweet 'n Low packet.

"Ah, yes, we are," I said. "Kids, what kind of cereal do you want?"

"Strawberry Bonkers," yelled one.

"Chocolate Zippies," yelled another.

"Fruity Tooties," yelled the third.

I turned to the waitress. "Three shredded wheat,

37

please." As the kids moaned, I replied, "You don't want to eat junk . . . it'll kill you."

"Oh, and, Miss, I'll have a large pastry and a bowl of coffee."

Rhonda ordered for herself and the baby, as I let my mind fantasize on that giant Bonzai Bun with all the hot butter, icing, and thirteen active ingredients to eat away your stomach lining. (What a way to go!)

One advantage to dry cereal is no waiting. So our waitress was right back with three small boxes of shredded wheat. The kids get a kick out of pouring the cereal from the box to the bowl. We're trying to bat .500. If there are thirty shredded wheat thingies in a box, we try to get fifteen in the bowl on the first try. We give an honorable mention if none get on the floor. We've never given an honorable mention.

I helped Joy and Jesse get settled and then turned to Jeffrey. Something was wrong. His cereal box was empty. So was his bowl.

"Jeffrey, where is your shredded wheat?" I asked.

"Right here," he said, pounding his shirt pocket.

"Don't pound your pocket . . . you're shredding your wheat!" Trying to reason with a two-year-old is pure comedy.

"Jeffrey, why did you put your shredded wheat in your pocket?" Rhonda asked.

" 'Cause it wouldn't all fit in my shoe."

Meanwhile the waitress brought Rhonda's eggs and my Bonzai Bun.

"Oh, no!" Rhonda shrieked. "What's that in the middle of your Bonzai Bun?"

I stared in equal horror and disbelief.

"Relax, Mom," soothed Jesse. "It's only my Wax Boy miniature action figure."

I wanted to turn *him* into Devious Dust, but I understand it's eight to ten in the slammer if you're a non-super hero.

Well, Joy and Jesse ate their dry cereal, Rhonda ate her eggs, I ate my Bonzai Bun (it tasted like wax), Jeffrey ate his shirt pocket, and John ate the scraps in his role as combination baby, dog, and garbage disposal.

After all the food was gone and all the liquid was spilled, we got up from our booth and went to pay our check.

As I handed the hostess the check, I tried to provide a little humor.

"Got change for a wet twenty?" I kidded.

Never cracking a smile, she gave me dry change and said with all the warmth of winter, "Have a nice day."

After breakfast, it was time for Phase Two. We went home, changed into dry clothes, and headed for the park. There's a great park near our house. It has a merry-go-round, a miniature train, a steamboat ride, a duck pond, and a few token ducks.

"Ah, the simple pleasures of life," Rhonda sighed.

I laughed to myself. "Simple?" I whipped out my pocket calculator to figure out what this simple pleasure was going to cost me.

"Let's see," I began. "There's tickets for the merry-go-round, tickets for the train, tickets for the boat, duck food, parking, taxes, title, and destination charges. This visit to the park is a major investment of funds!"

Rhonda gave me that "You're gonna have a good time with the kids or else" look. Suddenly money was no longer an issue.

The park was filled with kids and their fathers who felt guilty about not being with their kids so they went to the park to feel less guilty.

Only one problem . . . the park is boring.

"Well, let's pack it back into the car and head for home," I announced. "We'll come back again another Saturday for more high-powered fun, death-defying excitement, and frenzied ecstasy."

The kids nodded and yawned.

Home again after our park adventure, Joy and Jesse went out on their bikes and Jeffrey and John settled in for an afternoon nap.

Not a bad idea!

"Finally," sighed Rhonda. "Now we can get caught up on some household chores."

I looked at her as if *she* had just threatened to melt Wax Boy.

"Here's a little list I made," she said. "You'll be real proud of me. I'm getting organized."

In my dictionary, *organization* is a word that is only appropriate Monday through Friday. Organization takes the weekends off.

"Let me see your list," I mumbled.

"I ran out of scratch paper," she apologized. "So I wrote the list on paper towels."

"Okay, let me see the paper towel," I urged.

She handed me the whole roll.

"Oh, Rhonda, no . . . tell me it isn't true . . . the whole roll?"

"It's just little, two-minute jobs."

I started reading the list:

- Clean out the clothes closets
- Re-sod the lawn
- Wash the windows
- Fix the hole in the roof
- Rotate the tires on both cars

- Wallpaper the bathroom
- Dig up the roots to the oak tree in back
- Re-wire the house
- Sand and stain the end tables
- Enclose the back porch
- Plant a vegetable garden
- Panel our bedroom
- Install new plumbing
- Tune up the cars
- Put up a white picket fence
- Pour the concrete for a patio extension
- Add a second story

"Gee, if I'd seen this just an hour earlier, I could of had it done by dinner."

Rhonda had that "I'm gonna cry 'cause you're making fun of me" look.

"Don't cry. I wasn't making fun of you. Let's start out at the top of the list. We'll begin in the clothes closet."

It was full of junk. Our goal was to get a shirt into it. We settled for a tie.

I collapsed into a chair. As Saturday evening came upon us, I suddenly realized that in a few short hours it would be Sunday morning. That means getting four kids fed, scrubbed, dressed, and smiling in time for Sunday school.

Where did my day of rest go?

It's usually while I'm sitting in church Sunday morning, that I realize there will be plenty of Saturdays for "rest" down the road. I guess I can get by without that kind of rest right now in my life.

A day will come when I'll yearn for cartoons, carousels, cleaning, and, yes, even Wax Boy. And it will all be in the past.

I'm going to get all the satisfaction I can out of those times with my family. I'll sleep at a later date.

As a matter of fact, I'm reserving the year 2014 entirely for sleep. By then, I'll need it.

Get Me to the Church on Time

Every family with children has trouble getting ready for church. Ours seems to have more than most. So we have to be creative.

We have our own unique approach to this challenge: It was 3:45 A.M.

As the alarm went off, the clock radio announced that we were only fifteen minutes away from "The Sunrise Salvation Show," which would be aired in place of the usual "Farmer's Delight." Why the change in programming?

It was Sunday.

As a family we decided that the most Christian thing to do on Sunday is to make a stab at going to church. Going to church is okay, but scheduling it for Sunday

morning is a little overoptimistic. I've been really pushing our pastor for a Tuesday afternoon service instead,
so that we can all sufficiently recover from the weekend,
but apparently he's not listening.

Fortunately, our church has an early service and a
later service. To make the 9:00 A.M. early service, we
would have to begin preparing our family on Wednesday
evening. So, we decided to attend the 11:00 A.M. late (?)
service. That way, we can put off the initial stages of
preparation until Friday.

I know 3:45 A.M. is early, but I read once that astro-
nauts get up at 3:45 on the day of a launch . . . so I
thought that would be appropriate.

As I went through the barracks waking up the troops,
I was met by all manner of different reactions: Joy
stared through tired eyes and groaned; Jesse immediately started in on the questions of life (Why do we go to
bed when it's light, but wake up when it's dark? Are we a
family on the graveyard shift?). Jeffrey snorted at me as
he sucked his thumb and clung to his blanket. He was in
his preawake catatonic recline. John was up, pacing his
crib like a caged tiger. Yes, John had been awake for
hours, just waiting for the chance to be released from
his cribbed prison. See, part of the definition of *baby* is
one who sleeps when he shouldn't, never when he
should.

I returned to our bedroom to wake up the love of my
life.

"Whattya waking me up for at this hour, you dipstick?
I don't have the car pool today. I don't need to pack
lunches, they can eat in the school cafeteria! The kids
don't need breakfast, let them eat junk and watch TV!
They can dress themselves . . . make little signs for them
that say 'I AM COLOR-BLIND.' They know the

way to school, tell 'em I'll pick 'em up when school's out. Tell 'em to—"

"Wait, Dear," I interrupted. "It's not a school day. It's Sunday, we're going to church."

She cried, as she looked at her clock.

"Is this what it's like to be a missionary?" Rhonda moaned as she slowly made her way out of bed.

"No," I replied. "Missionaries don't go to church. They just take pictures and have them made into slide shows.

"By the way," I continued, looking at a woman who just woke up, "you'd make a great picture of a jungle native!"

Rhonda doesn't like "early morning looks" jokes. She was just about to throw a nightstand at me when the kids interrupted.

"If you don't feed us breakfast, we'll never make it to church. We'll die of malnutrition. Do you want everyone at church to see our bloated bellies? We'll look like a documentary on famine. Please feed us . . . *please!*"

"Knock off the dramatics," I yelled. "I'll fix you breakfast." As I left our bedroom I turned around for one last comment to Rhonda.

"Try to be an encouragement to the kids. Be positive about it being Sunday morning. Stress the *opportunity* and *privilege* we have in going to church."

"How's this?" Rhonda replied. "Cheer up, kids, it could be worse . . . it could be Monday!"

"That's really great, Babe," I answered weakly.

Out to the kitchen. It was *my* opportunity and privilege to prepare breakfast.

"What do you guys eat for breakfast?" I quizzed.

"Mama makes us bacon and eggs or homemade French toast or fresh oatmeal or some kinda omelette."

"Well then, let's see ... where do I begin?" I eagerly exclaimed, rubbing my hands together.

"Uhh ... Daddy ... are YOU gonna make us breakfast?"

"Yeah."

"We're not that hungry, then. We'll just eat crackers. You don't have to make us anything. Please, Daddy, don't cook us anything ... *please!*"

I checked the freezer. "How about if I toast you some frozen waffles?"

Joy whispered to Jesse, "I don't think he can ruin waffles ... it may be our best bet."

"Okay, Dad," Jesse answered. "That sounds terrific!" But he said it with all the excitement of an automatic transmission.

By then Rhonda walked in and brightly recited, "This is the day that the Lord hath made! Let us rejoice and be glad in it!"

Joy whispered to Jesse. "She's just doing that 'cause she feels bad about callin' Dad a dipstick."

Rhonda continued, "Well, you guys have fun praising God around the breakfast table. I'm gonna jump in the shower. ... By the way, it's time for 'The Sunrise Salvation Show' if anyone's interested! Just flip on the radio."

No one moved.

Suddenly there was a fragrance in the air much like that of the first day in chemistry class.

"What's that *gross* smell?"

I gasped, "It's the waffles in the toaster!"

The kids began to panic.

"Just stay calm everybody," I soothed. "I can put out that fire in a jiffy."

46

Our toaster oven looked like "The Towering Inferno."
I had to think fast. My first impulse was to use water . . .
but no, wait . . . you don't use water on a toaster with
burning waffles . . . or was it on a stove with burning
grease? . . . Anyway . . . I had to save the lives of my hor-
rified family.

I grabbed the canister of flour. I reached in, filled my
hand, and threw it on the toaster oven and burning waffles.

It looked like "The Towering Inferno Visits Antarc-
tica."

Nonetheless, the flour choked out the fire. Actually, I
believe it was the principle of displacement at work. The
toaster oven was so full of flour . . . there was no room for
a fire!

Underneath the white cloud, I peeled off four white
objects with pitch black undertones.

"Your waffles are ready!"

"Oh, Daddy, you're not gonna make us eat those
YUKKY waffles are you?"

"All right, let me get some of the flour off first, then
you'll enjoy them more."

I put each waffle under the spigot and tried to hose it
down. It didn't seem to work.

"Now, just put some yummy syrup on 'em and you're
all set," I smiled.

"Not even syrup can save this disaster," Jesse griped.

"Come on, kids, have a good attitude. Pretend the
flour is really powdered sugar!" I suggested. "We're
starting to run late!"

Jeffrey took a bite. "Daddy, it's *really* yukky. It tastes
like paste."

"It *is* paste," replied Joy.

"That's enough," I cried. "I did the best I could. Eat it

and don't complain ... Look at John, he's not making any noise. He's just eating nicely."

"His mouth is pasted shut."

"That's not a bad idea," I mused. "Now, eat your waffles and try not to get sticky."

"Look, Daddy, my waffle sticks to the wall all by itself!" Jeffrey exclaimed.

I guess I didn't turn around fast enough.

By the time I looked, not only was Jeffrey's waffle on the wall, but it was joined by both Joy's and Jesse's.

"This can't be happening to me," I cried in disbelief. "All because I wanted the family to go to church ... why, God?" I asked, looking up to the heavens.

John's waffle was on the ceiling.

"I'm out of the shower," Rhonda yelled. "It's the kids' bath time. Everyone in the tub! Hurry, it's getting late!"

"We can't, Mommy, we're stuck to our chairs!"

"No excuses, now. Daddy will help you while I get dressed."

"Peel me off, Dad," asked Jesse.

"Okay, kids," I ordered. "Get out of your pajamas. Leave them pasted to your seats. We gotta keep movin' or we'll be late to church. Now come on, I want you in the bathtub."

"Is everything going well on the Lord's day?" asked Rhonda, as she popped her head into the kitchen for a second.

Then she shrieked, "WHY IS JOHN BLUE?"

"He can't breathe, Mommy," Joy replied matter-of-factly. "His lips are pasted shut."

"Bath time, everyone!" I interrupted and grabbed John, heading for the tub.

Get Me
to the Church
on Time

In no time I de-pasted his mouth and he was back to normal—eating everything in sight.

"No fooling around in the tub today," I barked. "It's in and out so we can get you dressed. We need to be loading the car soon."

"Okay, Dad, we won't use all our bath toys."

I watched them dump in seven buckets of toys.

"No problem, Dad, we usually use eight!"

I honestly believed there were kids in that tub. But all I could see was boats, ducks, trucks, cars, elephants, army men, Weebles, Legos, Lincoln Logs, Smurfs, Strawberry Shortcake, Darth Vader, Yoda, Chewwy, E.T., and Wax Boy.

As I was looking at the toystore in a tub, I was thinking about how it seemed to be missing the two vital elements for an official bath: (1) people and (2) water.

Without warning I was suddenly showered by vital element number 2.

"What happened?" I dripped.

"My Junior Polaris Scale Model Underwater Self-Contained Missile Launcher just blasted off a beauty," Jesse rejoiced.

"But there's water all over the bathroom floor," I protested as I toweled off.

"Gee, Dad, we usually get water all over the HOUSE!"

"Well, not today, come on, everyone out of the tub, let's go." I hustled. I nervously glanced at my wet watch.

"But, Dad, we didn't get a chance to wash off. We haven't found the soap yet."

"I'm sorry, it's just too late now. If we don't keep moving we'll be late for church."

"Will we miss the kickoff?" Jeffrey asked.

"That's football, not church," corrected Joy. "If you're late for church, the rusher takes you down front and makes you sit on the first row. And you have to watch out, cuz if the pastor gets all excited, you get WET, cuz he—"

"Enough, Joy," I said sternly.

"Hi, Christian guys and gals!" It was Rhonda, smiling from ear to ear and looking like she used to be in Youth Work.

"It's time to get dressed," Rhonda continued.

"Honey," she said, "I'll get the girls ready, you get the boys ready."

"But, Rhonda," I protested. "We have one girl and three boys!"

"Well, whattya know."

Back in the boys' room I was faced with the age-old dilemma: What should the boys wear? They had to look neat, but they get so messy during Craft Times in Sunday school. I can't dress 'em too fancy . . . I may see my boss. I can't dress 'em too poorly . . . I may see my boss.

I decided to begin by dressing John. I quickly diapered him to avoid the risk of foreign substances in the atmosphere. I then attempted to put him in a little shirt and jumper set that looked so innocent on the hanger.

I put one arm through the appropriate sleeve. As I turned to the other arm, John systematically removed the shirt from the first arm.

We went through this process five times.

"Daddy doesn't want to break your little arm, Baby John," I began sweetly, "BUT I WILL IF NECESSARY!"

Once the shirt was on, it was time to button it. The buttons were the size of pinheads, and all of a sudden my hands looked as big as Johnny Bench's catcher's mitt.

"YOU NEED A DEGREE IN MICROSURGERY TO BUTTON THESE BUTTONS!!" I screamed.

"Is it time to leave, Dear?" Rhonda asked.

"We should have left ten minutes ago," I muttered.

I gave up and went for the jumper. I got one of his legs in and while I was working on the other. . . . Well, you know the story.

Meanwhile, Jesse and Jeffrey had taken a real weight off my shoulders.

They'd dressed themselves.

"I wanna wear a tie," Jeffrey announced.

"With a T-shirt?"

Jesse responded, "No problem, Dad, it's a clip-on."

I noticed that Jeffrey was wearing two different types of shoes and two different colored socks.

"Jeffrey, change your shoes and socks and put them on properly," I said. "I won't stand for sloppiness."

I was too busy to realize it, but all Jeffrey did was take the green sock off his left foot and put it on the right and vice versa with the shoes.

Jesse had on a pair of pants that made him look like he was trying to revive knickers. He observed me staring at his legs.

"Oh, Dad, I can't get these socks to pull up!"

"They're not supposed to go up over your knees, Son. Why not try wearing a longer pair of pants."

"That's a great idea, Dad!" he rejoiced.

I love being a creative consultant.

I checked the clock and saw that if I didn't start getting myself ready we'd never make it.

"I wonder if God forgives you if your son wears stripes and plaids together in public?" I pondered as I scurried into the shower.

Out of the shower and dressing, I was in high gear. Rhonda began the forty-minute process of getting kids strapped into car seats, buckled into regular seats, complete with blankets, bottles, diaper changes, Baby-Cleanums, powder, children's New Testaments, money for the missionaries, and a reminder to smile.

By now I was in the car and we were off.

Halfway to church, Joy reminded us, "Mama, your Bible is on the roof of the car!"

I screeched to a halt, hopped out, pulled her Bible off the roof (uncannily opened to Job), jumped back in, and once again sped off.

"Daddy, is it okay if you speed when we're going to church?"

"Daddy, if no one likes the front row of church, why do they all like the front row of the parking lot for their cars?"

"Why do we always have to dress up for church, Daddy? Are we 'sposed to be different on Sunday?"

All these questions left me at a total loss for words. *Well,* I thought to myself, *I guess that's one of the reasons we go to church . . . to get answers to our questions.*

Once we arrived at church, I gratefully observed that I was not the only person out of breath. As a matter of fact, there's a good chance that the person panting in the pew behind me was someone just like you. We all know the work involved in getting the crew to church.

But, in spite of all the hassle, it's worth it. There's something indescribable, almost mystical, about worship. What a welcome change of pace to quiet our spirits and turn our attention to our God.

As I bowed my head in prayer, I silently gave thanks to God for His unconditional acceptance of His children. This is always important to me, but that day it was especially meaningful. For as I concluded my prayer and opened my eyes, I discovered . . . I was wearing one blue sock and one green one.

Hospitality
May Be Hazardous
to Your Health

Do you have problems with kids and company? The night before people come over for dinner, do you toss and turn in your bed, imagining all the possible disasters? Does the thought of your crew sitting down to a formal meal conjure up the Boston Bruins at the ballet? As you recall previous attempts at a home of hospitality, do the flashbacks remind you of a World War I documentary?

Well, you're not alone, my friends. We've had our share of hospitality horrors.

As a matter of fact, when we invite people over for dinner, we have found it helpful to follow up the initial invitation with a series of disclaimers to protect us legally.

Anyone who agrees to have a meal with us in our house must understand the following rules:

- Enter at your own risk.
- Please lock your car. We are not responsible for lost or stolen valuables.
- Protect your hubcaps by removing them and securing them in your trunk.
- Wear clothing that is wash and wear.
- We are not liable for any form of personal injury, no matter how grotesque.
- The views expressed by the children do not necessarily reflect those of the management.
- Parental discretion is advised.
- Though this dinner has been edited for our guests, parts of it still may be too intense and explicit.
- You may be approached by religious fanatics passing out literature. They are not part of the family.
- Beware of low-flying children's toys.
- Warning: Do not operate this dinner without wearing safety goggles.
- We will supervise a body search of each child before you leave, thus assuring all is returned.
- We have the right to remain silent. Anything we say can be used against us in a court of law.
- We claim the right to have a lawyer present when being questioned.

Sure enough, when we mail out this disclaimer form to our dinner guests we find two things usually result:

1. We are legally protected.
2. We eat alone a lot.

Despite this warning, once we did have a couple agree to join us in our home for dinner. It was back when I was doing graduate study. One of my professors was extremely helpful in creating a program of study for me. I invited him and his wife to dinner.

They accepted.

The disclaimer didn't dull their anticipation. All I could figure is that they found our family to be a curious phenomenon. We'd make a great subject for a dissertation.

Well, everybody knows that there are two types of dinner guests. The one group consists of people who are just like you. Thus, dinner is as it always is. But the second group is made up of people you have to impress—like your boss, or your in-laws, or the pastor, or one of the kids' teachers.

The professor and his wife were definitely Group #2 material. Our goal was to wow them.

I got home from work early in order to be my usual helpful self. When I walked into the dining room, the table was already set.

"Man-oh-man, look at this!" I exclaimed. "We're even using plates and forks!"

Rhonda hustled right by me, ignoring my comment. "I can't find the cloth napkins. Please see if you can locate them and then set them up on each plate."

"CLOTH NAPKINS! Boy, who's comin' to dinner, the Pope?"

"Just find the napkins."

This was a lot harder than it sounded. We hadn't used cloth napkins since the time we thought Uncle Harry was coming to dinner. Uncle Harry died in 1961.

After franctially searching the house, I finally found them tucked between the souvenir beach towel from the 1964 New York World's Fair and the dish towels embossed with "I LIKE IKE."

Folding the napkins into a shape that would stand on a plate was the next challenge. I know they're all supposed to look alike, but as I folded each one I realized I was going to have to stress individuality.

Moving clockwise around our table setting for eight, the napkins looked like:

- Independence Hall
- the Matterhorn
- an upside-down ice cream cone
- the *Mayflower*
- a dugout canoe
- a split level
- Casper, the friendly ghost
- Louisiana

I knew all the kids would fight over Casper, but decided that Joy could sit with him, Jesse could sit by the Matterhorn, Jeffrey could dock by the *Mayflower*, and John would be over in the Louisiana territory.

"Okay, Sweetie, the napkins are all set up."

"Great, now could you do me a favor and make sure the living room is still tidy?"

As I walked back into the living room I realized that when you have four kids, tidy is always in the past tense.

"Kids!" I yelled. "Get in here and help me clean up this mess!"

"They can't, Dear," Rhonda interrupted. "They have to get dressed. If they don't get dressed now, they'll never be ready in time for the guests. You want them ready, don't you?"

"Okay, okay," I mumbled as I got down on my hands and knees. *Look at me,* I thought to myself. *Here I am a grown man and I'm down on the floor picking up dolls, Star Wars men, trucks, blocks, and other assorted juvenile trivia.*

"Honey," I said, "I'll finish the living room in a few minutes. I want to talk to the kids about something."

I walked into the boys' room. They were trying their best to dress themselves, but it looked a little like a psychedelic revival of the sixties.

"Here, Jeffrey, why not wear these nice dark blue pants instead of those orange plaid ones. I think Dr. and Mrs. Bain will like these better."

"Blue is yukky," Jeffrey replied.

"No, orange plaid is yukky ... especially with a red paisley shirt.

"Now listen to me, Sons," I said as I called them together.

"Daddy, you only call us Sons when you're gonna yell," Jesse observed.

"Well, I'm not going to yell," I stated. "I'm going to make a few *suggestions* about dinner tonight."

Jesse then whispered to Jeffrey, "Oh-oh, it's Group #2 company. This will be murder."

"That's enough, Jesse. Dr. and Mrs. Bain from the university are coming over for dinner. Now I don't want you boys to pull any surprises. I want you to be well-behaved little boys. I want you to sit quietly, speak only when spoken to, be neat, be helpful, and let's try to have a nice *normal* meal, okay?"

As they nodded their heads, I knew what a judge must feel like as he sentences a criminal to life in prison.

I finished dressing the boys and started into Joy's room when, all of a sudden, terror struck our home. It

was panic in the raw, unfathomable fear, chilling desper-
ation, psychological trauma ... the doorbell rang.

"AHHHHHHHHHHHHHH," shrieked Rhonda.
"THEY'RE HERE ALREADY!!!"

I glanced at my watch. "Six-thirty ... right on time."

"Don't they know that on time is early," said Rhonda,
continuing to panic.

"Relax, Babe. It's gonna be all right." I decided I
needed to take command.

"Joy, take John and keep him busy. Jeffrey, go comb
your hair. Jesse, go to the door and let the Bains in. I'll
pick up the toys in the living room. Everyone smile and
be sweet, or Daddy will belt you!"

Everyone took their appropriate positions. As I was
scurrying around jamming toys under the sofa, love seat,
recliner, and chair, I overheard Jesse greeting our
guests.

"Hi, you guys, come right on in. Mom's in the kitchen
cookin' junk, and Dad's in the living room all by himself
playing with our toys down on the floor."

Before I could get up, I was caught. They walked right
in to see me throwing Betsy Wetsy under the love seat
cushion and jamming Obi Wan Kenobi into my pants
pocket.

"Well, hello," I said from my hands and knees, trying
to stand up.

"No, no, don't get up for us," said Mrs. Bain, as her
husband pulled out a notebook and began writing fever-
ishly.

"Please, won't you sit down?" I asked as I went for the
love seat.

I didn't want them to sit on Betsy Wetsy.

"We'll be eating in just a few moments," I continued
politely.

"That's just fine," replied Mrs. Bain.

Hospitality
May Be Hazardous
to Your Health

Dr. Bain just stared and wrote, stared and wrote.

"I combed my hair all by myself," announced Jeffrey as he walked in. "I used a comb, a brush, water, hair spray, and shampoo."

It was obvious.

His hair made him look like a demented cross between Bozo the Clown and a Caesar salad. The mixture provided his hair with the uncanny ability to stick straight out yet, at the same time, drip.

"Uhh, this is my son Jeffrey," I stammered.

"Hi," Jeffrey continued. "Want me to sit on your lap?"

I quickly grabbed Jeffrey and sent him to the kitchen to help Rhonda. I just couldn't stand that look of fear on the faces of the Bains.

Quickly changing the subject, I spoke to Dr. Bain, "So tell me, Dr. Bain, how are things at the university?"

He was so embroiled in his note taking, he never heard a word.

"Things are quite exemplary, thank you," Mrs. Bain replied in place of her absentee husband.

"Daddy, Daddy, I tried my best."

It was Joy. She sounded defeated.

"I kept John real quiet in my room, but he started playing with my Magic Markers."

"Is he drawing with them?" I asked.

"No, he's eating them."

Next thing I knew, out into the living room crawled John.

He looked like a multicolored sacrifice to the god of the rainbow.

"This is our baby, John," I introduced. "I'll just wash him off real quick."

"No good, Dad . . . it's permanent ink."

SQUISH, SQUASH, SQUISH, SQUASH, Jeffrey

walked back in, still wet from combing his hair. "Dinner's ready! Come and eat Mommy's yukky food!"

"Ha, ha, ha, oh, those kids," I faked my way through a laugh, holding in my arms the human color chart. "Let's go over to the table."

I quickly shackled John to his high chair, boosted Jeffrey into his booster chair, and put Joy and Jesse in their seats.

Jesse looked at Dr. Bain and said, "You go eat by Independence Hall and she gets to eat by a dugout canoe."

Mrs. Bain dropped her jaw.

Dr. Bain was on his third notebook.

I tried to save the situation. "Jesse thinks your napkins look like Independence Hall and a dugout canoe. He's an incredibly creative little guy."

"He's incredible all right," sighed Mrs. Bain.

Rhonda brought in the last of the goodies. I finally took the opportunity to introduce her.

"This is my wife, Rhonda. This is Dr. and Mrs. Bain."

"It's so nice to have you in our home," Rhonda smiled sweetly.

Mrs. Bain got up, grabbed Rhonda by the shoulders, looked her straight in the eye, and said, "HONEY, YOU ARE ONE BRAVE WOMAN!"

She once again gained her composure and took her seat.

When we were all seated I said, "We usually pray before our meal. We thank God for the food."

"Yeah, if Daddy cooks, we also ask for healing."

"That's enough, Jesse," I politely snapped. I pinched him under the table. Jeffrey yelled, "OUCH!"

So I bowed my head to pray. I noticed that the kids kept their eyes open.

Joy pointed to the Bains and whispered to Jesse,

"Let's see if they close their eyes." I pinched Joy under the table. John yelled, "OUCH!"

"Dear Lord, thank You for our friends and this food. Amen."

"You prayed long tonight, Daddy."

We began to pass around the food. The kids couldn't resist making editorial comments on each dish.

"Don't eat this, it's GROSS."

"This is a YUKKY VEGETABLE. We hold our noses when we eat it."

"After I eat this stuff, I feel like—"

"Children, please!"

During the entire meal Jeffrey was staring constantly at Mrs. Bain. He was sitting right next to her so it was quite obvious. Finally he revealed his heart.

"Lady, I like you."

We all smiled sweetly as we saw his bright eyes conveying his crush on our guest.

Then, in a gesture of love, he laid his little head on Mrs. Bain's arm. "You're a nice lady," he said.

The problem was not with Jeffrey, but with Mrs. Bain's arm.

It was starting to drip shampoo onto her plate.

Well, up to this point, everything was verbal. It was now time for action.

It all started very innocently, for no reason, without any premeditation or forethought, and by no malice of her own . . . Joy suddenly fell out of her chair.

She was on the floor, flat on her face.

To say she was embarrassed is to put it mildly.

"Come on back up, Joy, it's okay," I soothed.

"No . . . no . . . I won't . . . I won't." Joy was now under the table, hiding out.

"Joy, please. It's okay. I'm sure we've all fallen out of

our chairs for no apparent reason. Joy, please come back up."

She wouldn't listen.

So I reached down to pinch her. Rhonda yelled, "OUCH!"

While we were down under the table, trying to reason with Joy, we suddenly heard a new and different sound coming from Multi-Color Man.

John was in his high chair gagging on his food.

So Rhonda was trying to reason with Joy, I was trying to save John's life, Jeffrey was dripping shampoo on Mrs. Bain, Dr. Bain was taking copious notes.

Where was Jesse?

He had made a quick trip to his room, but he was back, complete with hat and cane. Yes, you guessed it, folks, he was not going to be upstaged.

He was standing on his chair doing a little Fred Astaire for everyone's dining and dancing pleasure.

I lifted my head from under the table to see this dripping, hiding, gagging, dancing mess, we call "having guests for dinner."

I tried to get control of Jesse by pinching him. Dr. Bain jumped, then wrote even more furiously.

"We've had a lovely evening," Mrs. Bain yelled over the confusion. "Bernard needs to arise early tomorrow so we must be going."

I looked at my watch.

It wasn't even 7:00 P.M. yet.

"Come, Bernard, let's be going."

"Well . . . well . . . thank you for coming . . . uhh . . . let me see you to the door . . ." I was really stumbling.

"No, that won't be necessary. Good evening."

They were gone.

We dripped, gagged, danced, and stared in disbelief.

Finally, I spoke.

"I just can't believe this."

Jesse answered, "Why not, Dad?"

I just stared.

"You told us before they came that you wanted to have a *normal* meal. Well, that's what we had, one of our *normal* meals."

Everyone went about their routines while I remained comatose. It was just too incredible to be true. The more I thought of it, the more I realized how right Jesse was.

This *was* a normal meal for our crew. Mealtime is a time for family fun. It's not Stuffed Shirt City. What was to be proved by radically changing our life-style for this one meal? How hypocritical could I get, eating one way with one group and another way with another ... especially when it's *our home.*

Well, as I think back over that occasion, I make some important discoveries.

Before I can really reach out and minister through hospitality, I've got to learn to accept myself and my family just the way we are. There's no need for hypocritical "shows" for the sake of impressing our guests. What they see is what they get!

If my kids see the same "me" in front of guests that they see when it's just our family, I think they'll learn a valuable lesson in being real.

And being real is what it's all about.

By the way, I did make one other discovery as I remembered that dinner . . . .

I think I know why I never got my graduate degree.

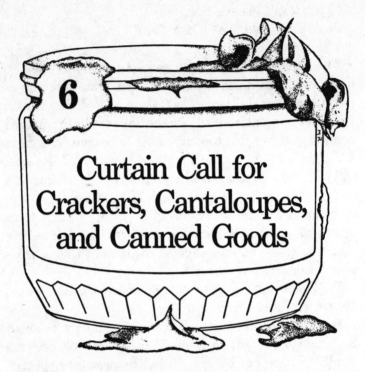

6

Curtain Call for Crackers, Cantaloupes, and Canned Goods

What do you do for entertainment? Some people are into the country club scene. Others are into TV. Some enjoy the movies. Still others buy cable TV in order to be into TV and movies at the same time. Some play at tennis, bowling, racquetball, golf, or horseshoes. Some hit the beach or the mountains. Some go out to eat, or to a ball game, or to a concert. What do *I* do for entertainment?

I go to the grocery store—and I take the kids along.

There's no question in my mind that the grocery store is the world's most entertaining establishment. Buying food is merely an aside. I go to watch the people.

I go first class. I take the kids with me to provide further frivolity and also to give Rhonda some temporary sanity at home.

We can feel the anticipation building even as we enter the parking lot. Most of the shoppers are quiet, unassuming, reserved women. But when they hit the parking lot, they turn into Godzilla.

There were twenty-seven available parking spaces on the *side* of the store. Yet one and only one spot was really desirable: the spot *in front of* the store. There was a car in it, but the lady was putting her groceries in her trunk, so it would become available momentarily.

Seven women had their sights fixed on that one coveted parking place. They jockeyed their cars into position. The little compact cars had the advantage in weaving and squirming. Station wagons, vans, and the '57 Buick with the fins had the advantage of intimidation. No one wants to get kissed by an old Buick.

Everyone waited nervously for the lady to load up her car. It appeared that she had purchased enough food to feed Yugoslavia through July.

At last, she was finished.

She hopped in and started the car. Our sweaty palms gripped our steering wheels even more tightly. This was the moment of truth.

We all knew that much would be determined by her exit pattern. Would she back up and turn left? That would give the advantage to the Toyota. However, if she backed out and turned right, it would be a battle between a Ford van and our finned friend, the '57 Buick.

She turned right.

What happened next is a blur in my mind's eye. There was a flurry of feathers, fenders, fluff, Fords, and fins. Tires screeched, horns honked, fists flew, transmissions transmitted.

As the dust cleared, the winner emerged.

As I said, it's all a blur to me. For the life of me, I can't figure out how the Toyota got the spot.

As we entered the store we saw the same battle in miniature as we all participated in "Fight for Your Shopping Cart." Everyone had their sights set on the shiny one. It was a mad dash. Once again our heroine in the Toyota emerged victorious (even without her Toyota!).

But vengeance is sweet. Her cart was stuck to another one.

We all passed by her with a smile, knowing justice had been served.

The first aisle is canned goods, juices, and salad dressings. This is a busy aisle because people are still getting into the grocery groove. By the time we get to Aisle 5, they'll be moving like a finely tuned machine.

The first person we saw in Aisle 1 must have been a professional juggler. In her two tiny hands, she was balancing a seven-page shopping list, a pencil, a pen, a checkbook, a wallet, keys, coupons, newspaper ads from other stores, three back issues of *Consumer Reports,* a set of rosary beads, and her own personal computer.

Next we ran into your typical housewife with your typical eight-year-old son. He was playing that famous grocery store game: "How Much Stuff Can I Put Into the Cart Without Parental Permission?" This is a great game, but it causes real bottlenecks at the checkout counter.

"Joy, can you put two bottles of apple juice in the cart for me please?" I asked.

"But, Dad, Angie Dickinson says on TV you can save forty-two cents a bottle if you buy no-name, generic, plain-brown-wrap, bag-and-bottle-your-own-stuff, squeezed-from-a-seed brand!"

"Okay, we'll wait till we get to that aisle then."
couldn't help but wonder what kind of apple juice Angie
Dickinson really drinks.

On to Aisle 2, where we saw cake mixes, soups, teas,
coffee, sugar, flour, and spices. We noticed the lady from
the '57 Buick in front of the cake mixes. As she loaded
them into her cart we concluded that her goal was to
look like her car.

Up by the tea we saw this really way-out type, grilling
the stock boy about herbal tea.

"What do you mean you don't have Sunshine Tapioca
Treebark Royal Root Tea?" she snapped. "I bet your
competitor has it!"

"Only if his store is in China, Lady," responded a
weary tea stacker.

Around the corner was Aisle 3. It was as if we were
miraculously transported into a world of color and cartoons. Yes . . . we were in the cereal aisle.

This is the point where the kids really come alive.
Every cereal has its own angle: Some have cartoon characters on the box like Tarzan, Bozo, Captain Crisp,
Super Hero Slop, Space Age Sparkles, and even Lassie
(although I think she belongs in Aisle 5).

Another angle is a cereal's shape. Besides your garden
variety flakes, there are puffs, pops, shreds, chex, hexa-
gons, pentagons, trapezoids, rhombuses, donuts, pastries, footballs, boats, 747s, and of course every grown
man's fantasy—cereal shaped like flowers.

Finally there's a cereal's color. Less and less cereal is
your basic golden brown. Now there's blue, pink, green,
orange, yellow, red, purple, white, peach, chocolate
brown, mauve, aquamarine, persimmon, turquoise, and
fuchsia.

I'm waiting for a cereal that's solid black.

Anyway this aisle was filled with kids promising their parents they would do anything if they could just have a box of purple trapezoids with Anthracite the Rock Man on the front of the box. Most mothers eventually wore down, so many of the shopping carts had a box of these Grape Granites in them.

Past the kiddie cereals we entered "Natural Country." I could tell we were getting close because there were two ladies in jogging suits, running in place in front of the Granola.

They were having a discussion over the difference between *high fiber* and *roughage*.

It was not the kind of discussion I wanted my kids to hear. So, I grabbed the old faithful box of shredded wheat and headed on down the aisle.

"Daddy, did you eat shredded wheat when you were a kid?" Jeffrey asked.

"Yes, Jeffrey, as a matter of fact I did."

Jesse piped in, "I think President Lincoln ate shredded wheat, didn't he, Dad?"

"Well, I'm not sure," I hedged. "But I know he didn't eat Grape Granites."

We turned again and entered Aisle 4. I can always tell this aisle from the others, because the people here are all victims of impulse buying.

These people hustle into the store and right down Aisle 1 saying to themselves, *I don't need a shopping cart. I'm only getting a couple of items.*

Well, by the time they hit Aisle 4 their personages are overflowing with the broadest definition of a "couple of items" I've ever seen.

So there's always a lot of food on the floor in Aisle 4.

The store keeps a boy with a mop on this aisle full-time.

Curtain Call for
Crackers, Cantaloupes,
and Canned Goods

Aisle 4 is the bread aisle. I like to see people's initial reactions when they see an *entire aisle* devoted to bread.

Sure enough, there was a ten-year-old boy lamenting to his friend, "Mom wanted me to get a loaf of bread. Holy mackerel, there must be fifty different kinds!"

It was a veritable worldwide excursion as he looked at bread from every country on this planet.

"Well, shall we get African Green Bread or West Indies Whole Wheat?" the boy's friend asked.

"Here, let's get this one," the boy decided, picking up a loaf of Australian Bush Bread.

I'd love to have seen his mother's reaction when he got home with a loaf of bread endorsed by aborigines.

Pet food is the main attraction in Aisle 5. This is where one can see some real seasoned veterans of the shopping world.

They've usually filled one cart already, so now they're wielding two carts. You can pretty much tell how much pet food they'll put in the second cart by listening to them talk about their pet.

If they want to buy the right dog food for Fifi, Teeny, Juanita, or Squirt, you know it won't be much food.

But when you hear them discussing the right food for Bruiser, Butkus, Bruno, or Brutus, then you know the second cart will be full of dog food and they'll be bringing along a neighbor to push cart number three.

Three-cart people deserve a medal for bravery, stamina, and endurance. Sometimes it can take four days before they get out of the store.

The next aisle was overflowing with stock boys. People were staring in bewilderment, wondering why an army of employees were stocking soap, cleaners, bleach, and detergent. Most people admitted, they'd never seen this many stock boys on one aisle at one time. What was the reasoning behind the Stock Boy Convention on Aisle 6?

"I know what's going on," I announced, having seen this natural phenomenon take place before.

"What is it, then?" the people inquired. "Oh, please tell us ... please!"

"The explanation is very simple," I began. "I predict that if you go down to the other end of the aisle, you'll discover a very pretty girl with very little on!"

One brave soul waded through the maze of cartons, cardboard, and cleanser. Suddenly a joyous yelp came from the other end of the aisle, "You're right, you're right!" he rejoiced. "She's a beauty, too!" he added.

So remember, when you see an aisle loaded with stock boys:

1. Somewhere on the aisle is a pretty girl.

2. Thus, all the shelves are stocked with the wrong products.

We finally came to the no-name, generic, plain-brown-wrap, mystery-brand, bag-and-bottle-it-yourself aisle ... conveniently abbreviated to Aisle 7. Once again, however, we found the shelves were stocked with the wrong products. There were brand names all over the place.

Yet it's important to point out that this was not the fault of the stock boys. This was a consumer-caused complication.

We stood back and watched this problem reenacted: Along came your basic shopper with two giant-size jars of peanut butter in her cart. She paused at the no-name aisle long enough to notice that the no-name peanut butter is obviously cheaper. So what did she do?

She took the brand-name peanut butter out of her cart and put it on the no-name shelf in order to make room in her cart for the fifty-five-gallon drum of plain-wrap peanut butter!

As we scanned the aisle, we saw that this had been the case for most every product. There were bags of brand-name spaghetti in place of brown-wrap crates ... there were six-packs of soft drinks like Coke and Pepsi in place of no-frills five-liter jugs ... even brand-name paper towels instead of plain-wrap paper by the ream.

I dug back behind all the bottles of brand-name apple juices in order to find Angie Dickinson's recommendation. I found one lone bottle at the very back of the shelf. As I pulled it out, I saw a label on the side that said, "Best if used before this date ...."

I dusted off the label to see the date and realized I was holding a bottle of apple juice that was older than Angie Dickinson's mother.

We skipped Aisle 8 because it was hair care, lotions, and remedies. I've always thought that it's better to buy those things at a drugstore. I don't buy junk food at a pharmacy even though it makes me sick. Why should I buy bicarbonate at the grocery store?

I feel a deeper sense of loyalty this way.

Passing Aisle 8, we entered the outer edges of subzero wasteland ... frozen foods.

I've always been fascinated by the frozen food stock boy. First off, he's not a boy. He's a man, obviously meeting the requirement of fifteen years' experience in the frozen tundra of Greenland. Everyone else shivers and moves briskly through this aisle of ice; yet he just stands there in his short sleeves and faithfully stocks shelves with frozen, French-cut green beans.

As the shoppers walk by this man, they do so with respect. He's a testimony to clean-living, Popsicle-licking, John Wayne-loving America.

Whenever I pass him, I salute.

I attempted to enter the meat aisle, but by then I was so cold from the frozen food aisle, I couldn't stand one more aisle of numbness.

Personally, I think this is why a lot of people have become vegetarians. They can't stand the temperatures in the meat aisle.

Our last aisle was a fitting climax to our show—the produce aisle. Before rushing in, we stood back to get an overview. It really was a sight. There was so much pinching, squeezing, coddling, tapping, knocking, bouncing, smelling, shaking, eyeing, drying, bagging, weighing, throwing, pushing, pulling, grating, and blending, I felt I was in a food processor being pureed.

As my eye scanned the crowd, I realized we were not going to make it. One lady was determined to find the best head of lettuce in the whole pile . . . and of course, she was convinced that head was at the bottom.

Just as I expected, all of a sudden there was an eruption from Mount Produce as a bed of flowing, lavalike, iceberg lettuce settled at the feet of those trapped in the produce aisle.

One natural disaster usually leads to another. The lettuce triggered off the cantaloupes, followed by grapefruit (pink and yellow), tomatoes, tangerines, and onions.

It soon spread to Idaho and there were potatoes all over the aisle.

It finally hit broccoli. But you know, you just don't move broccoli. It's not a real rollable object.

Our eyes welled up with tears of joy when we saw those brave stalks of raw broccoli saving us from possible destruction.

We made our way safely to the front of the store in preparation for checkout. There are fourteen checkout counters (obviously built for no-waiting), yet there were only three counters open.

No matter what time of day or night you check out, there will always be eleven employees at lunch or on break.

Of the three counters that were open, only two were really available because the third one is for "10 items or less."

I don't even consider that counter, because I once saw a woman try to check out eleven items in that line. I've heard about wars, natural disasters, mutilations, cruel tortures, and hideous exterminations. But I've *never* seen or heard anything as gory as what they did to that lady. The eleven items still stand by the counter to this day as a memorial to one who tried and failed.

Now we were up to the counter and it was time to unload. This store has those newfangled scanner systems that ring up your groceries by computer. The checkout lady ran my apple juice over the scanner . . . no "beep." She tried it again and again, and again. Finally it "beeped" on the fifth try. (By the way, when I got home I found I'd been charged for five bottles of apple juice.)

They don't use paper bags at this store anymore either. They use those new plastic imitations that start out the size of a candy bar, yet will ultimately hold the entire canned food aisle.

It's depressing to pay all that money for groceries and carry home only two bags.

"The total is $67.48," said the girl who works for the scanner.

I pulled out my checkbook and heard groans all the way down the line. The little checkout gal started her thing:

"Driver's License?"

"Major Credit Card?"

"Social Security Number?"

"Highest Year of Schooling?"

"Number of Dependents?"

"Average Annual Income Computed Over Last Five Years?"

By now the manager had been called to the check-stand to decide if I was writing a valid check. He looked over the check, looked over me, frisked me, then okayed the purchase.

When we walked back to our car and began to load our groceries into the backseat, we noticed that the lady with the Toyota was preparing to leave her coveted parking spot at the front of the store.

What happened next is still somewhat of a blur in my mind's eye. There was a flurry of feathers, fenders, fluff, Fords, and fins. Tires screeched, horns honked, fists flew, transmissions transmitted.

As the dust cleared, a new winner emerged . . . as does the moral—man does not live by Grape Granites (or parking spaces) alone.

My First
Camping Trip

Some people like camping out. You may be one.

My idea of camping is the Marriott or, if I really want
to rough it, a Holiday Inn. Unfortunately, my family and
friends don't see it that way so I was in for an educational experience.

It all started out innocently enough. My friend Paul
invited Joy, Jesse, and myself to spend the night camping on the beach. He was bringing his four-year-old,
James, and he had also invited Fred and his four-year-
old, Adam, as well as Bob and his four-year-old, Amy.

I couldn't imagine all these kids at a brunch at the
Marriott, but decided to give it a try. I should have sus-
pected something when he told us to bring sleeping bags.

"Don't the maids work on weekends?" I kidded.

Paul just stared blankly.

You've got to know my background to understand. I have a lack of wilderness experience. I was once lost in the sporting goods department at Penneys, but that's about it.

The plan was for Paul and Bob to drive down early and "set up camp." (I thought that meant check in.) Fred and I would come down later, after Fred got off work.

As we got closer and closer to our destination, something was becoming crystal clear . . . the Marriott was a myth.

"Think of all the money we're saving," commented Fred, as we approached the entrance to the campground.

"That's eighteen dollars a night for the campsite, plus four dollars per vehicle," growled Ranger Rita. "Will you be driving in and out of the campground?"

We nodded.

"Okay, then add on a four-dollar reentry fee."

All I could think of was the fact that the Marriott never charged for reentry.

"All right, you guys are in Slot 96. Go down to the men's outhouse, turn left, and you'll see it on your right."

"Oh, that's good news, we're right near the bathroom!" Fred was genuinely encouraged.

I tried to look gratified, but I was inwardly concluding that Fred was a sadist.

We drove in and found Bob, Paul, and kids all set up in Slot 96. They had already pitched (that's camping lingo, not baseball) three tents and were busy lighting the fire for dinner.

"Welcome, Campers!" greeted Paul cheerily.

The five kids all congregated to set their plans for high adventure.

I was calling upon the Lord to be saved.

"Bill, why don't you find some long sticks for us to use in cooking our hot dogs," suggested Bob.

As I went out on my stick search, I assessed the situation. "Here I am at a campground, preparing to eat hot dogs off a stick, and then sleep in a tent—in a sleeping bag."

I quickly confessed all known sin and vowed to love God forever.

When I returned, the kids were having a blast, climbing trees and running freely. Paul, Bob, and Fred were kicked back and laughing contagiously.

Since I couldn't find any sticks, we had to improvise.

"Everybody grab a coat hanger, straighten it out, and stab a weenie!" Paul yelled.

I just kept thinking of beef-kabob over a bed of rice pilaf with a side of green beans almondine.

"Here's your buns, Dad!" quipped Jesse, as he threw me a couple of rolls in which to hide my hot dogs.

"Thanks, Son," I replied. I noticed everyone's hot dogs looked nice and golden brown, while mine looked like the result of arson.

"There's nothing like hot dogs cooked over an open fire," sighed Bob.

I had to agree. There was *nothing* quite like what I was eating.

It began to get dark, so we kept the fire going. As soon as the dinner dishes were cleaned up (that means throw everything into the fire), we all sat around the campfire singing songs and telling stories.

I couldn't get comfortable to save my life. I'm really

My First
Camping Trip

not a sit-on-the-ground person. I kept wishing I'd packed my recliner.

While everyone else looked totally relaxed I was sitting, leaning, laying, propping, stretching, rolling, crouching, and finally standing.

The kids all took turns telling their favorite stories and shouting out their favorite songs. I kept looking at my watch, hoping everyone would soon be as tired as I.

Eventually the glorious hour arrived ... bedtime.

We got the kids ready and decided they could all sleep in the same tent. The tent was small, but we packed them in. While putting Joy and Jesse into their sleeping bags, I got both of their pajamas stuck in their respective sleeping bag zippers.

At least I could be sure they wouldn't wander off in the night.

With all the kids securely zipped into bags and tent, the four men gathered around the campfire to man-talk. I noticed Fred and Bob were teary-eyed.

"Boy, you guys are really emotional about this whole camping scene," I commented.

"No, it's hay fever," they replied in unison. "And neither one of us brought any medicine."

I volunteered to drive into town and buy their medication. Fred refused, choosing to "gut it out." Bob jumped at the chance.

"We'll be right back," waved Bob as we drove off.

After four hours at a campsite, we drove to the next best thing after a Marriott ... a 7-Eleven.

Bob bought medicine. I bought coffee. *Things always look better after a cup of coffee,* I thought to myself.

So I was wrong.

We drove back to camp, sat around the campfire (make that three sat, one stood), looked at the stars, swatted bugs, wallowed in dirt, smelled like smoke from the campfire, and generally went through the motions of having a great time.

I was yawning, Fred and Bob were sneezing, wheezing, and honking, Paul was staring blankly.

We finally decided to call it a night. I suggested we let Wheezer and Sneezer sleep in the same tent, but Paul was already set up with Bob the Wheezer, so I was left with Sneezy.

I felt like Dopey.

I unrolled my sleeping bag and looked for the pillow I had assumed accompanied each bag.

"There's no pillow in my sleeping bag."

"That's right," sneezed Fred. "You have to bring one along if you want one."

"Of course," I said, realizing that it was just me and the good earth.

Fred entered the tent, unrolled his bag, hopped into it, and then zipped up the mosquito netting by the front of the tent.

"We don't want any unexpected guests in the middle of the night," he laughed.

I gulped.

Bob and Paul had set up the tent on a patch of sloping land. I didn't want to sleep with my head far below my feet, so I slept with my feet downhill and my head uphill . . . right by the tent flap.

"Oops, I better go check on Adam one more time before I turn in," Fred said.

He unzipped the netting which was right by my head: Z Z Z Z Z Z Z Z Z Z Z Z I P. It sounded like the world's loudest zipper. It was.

No sooner had I recovered from the first blast of noise, than Fred hustled back in and rezipped the netting.

Z Z Z Z Z Z Z Z Z Z Z Z Z Z I P !

I never knew a zipper and a 747 could have so much in common.

So here I was trying to doze off, sleeping on a mattress of granite, with a guy on the other side of the tent gasping for air through hay-fevered lungs.

Suddenly Fred lifted his head. "What's that noise?"

"I don't hear anything," I mumbled weakly.

"I think it's an animal. I'll go check."

Z Z Z Z Z Z Z Z Z Z Z Z Z Z I P !

"Thanks," I mumbled, sleep still avoiding me.

Z Z Z Z Z Z Z Z Z Z Z Z Z Z I P !

"I think it was a skunk, but I chased it off."

I felt safe, knowing that if an animal were to attack our tent, Fred could sneeze it away.

By that time I was really drowsy. I was really ready to doze when Fred's voice cut into the silence.

"You know what? It's the trash cans out by Slot 95. That's what the skunk was after. I think I'll move those cans and then we won't be disturbed by little creatures again!"

Z Z Z Z Z Z Z Z Z Z Z Z Z Z I P !

Fred was once again out of the tent.

It was like trying to sleep through a Mick Jagger performance.

Z Z Z Z Z Z Z Z Z Z Z Z Z Z I P !

"There, that should take care of the trash problem."

I figured that peace of mind would lull Fred to sleep; but it didn't. It became increasingly apparent that the hay fever was taking its toll on the old boy. He was wheezing and honking like a Model A until he finally gave in to it.

"I've gotta go to Bob's tent and get some medicine or I'll never get to sleep."

Z Z Z Z Z Z Z Z Z Z Z Z Z I P !

I was beginning to think "never getting to sleep" was part of the definition of camping.

Fred got his pill and scurried back to our tent.

Z Z Z Z Z Z Z Z Z Z Z Z Z I P !

I was just about to ask Fred to leave the netting unzipped. Being eaten by a wild animal could be no more torturous than what I was enduring.

I didn't get my suggestion out because a cry came from the children's tent.

"That's Adam," Fred yelled as he bolted up and out.

Z Z Z Z Z Z Z Z Z Z Z Z Z I P !

By this time I was making a mental list of things I hated. I thought to myself, *I hate camping, I hate hay fever, I hate ZIPPERS.*

Z Z Z Z Z Z Z Z Z Z Z Z Z I P !

"Adam's okay."

We both settled in for some shut-eye. (That's another good camping expression. You don't sleep, just shut eyes.)

This time I was so close to dreamland I could see the entrance.

"Daddy, let me sleep with you. I don't wanna sleep with the kids." It was Adam at our tent flap.

"Okay, Adam, but be quiet so we don't wake up Bill."

Z Z Z Z Z Z Z Z Z Z Z Z Z I P !

"Here, sleep in here in my sleeping bag."

Z Z Z Z Z Z Z Z Z Z Z Z Z I P !

Having youth in the tent brought a whole new dimension to interruptions.

"Dad, I gotta go to the bathroom."

Z Z Z Z Z Z Z Z Z Z Z Z Z I P !

It was like a horror show. And it was happening to me.

Fred and Adam returned from the outhouse.

85

Z Z Z Z Z Z Z Z Z Z Z Z Z Z I P !

It was at this point that Fred delivered the classic line of the camp-out:

"This zipper isn't bothering you, is it, Bill?"

It was like that all night. I guess it averaged out to an unzippering every twenty minutes with a rezipping every ten.

I never did get to sleep.

Soon the sun was up and so were the kids.

Paul and Bob emerged from their tent well rested. Fred and I looked like two patrons of the local rescue mission.

I stumbled down to the outhouse to try and get cleaned up. But there's only so much you can do in one breath.

I must admit that I was embarrassed by the fact that Bob, Paul, and Fred all had a day's growth of beard. I get a day's growth of beard once every March and September and here we were smack in the middle of May.

So I convinced everyone that I had shaved in the outhouse. They all thought I was a neatness freak instead of a man with a preadolescent face.

We ate a he-man camper's breakfast. It consisted of coffee cakes and pastries made by the wives before we left civilization. After having lived fifteen hours on two black dogs, this food tasted heavenly.

After breakfast it was time to "break down camp." (You know, check out, turn in your key, grab your hat.) I was in charge of putting our tent back into a small canvas backpack. I felt this was unfair since I had not seen it leave the backpack and turn into a tent, but my arguing was futile.

So I pulled up stakes and wound up ropes and yanked apart poles and folded up canvas and did the best I could to get it all into the backpack. Unfortunately, I didn't even come close. (I learned later I should have removed the sleeping bags first.)

We got everything packed up and back into the cars. The kids looked sad to see the camp-out end. As I looked into their eyes I saw why camp-outs were created. It's that look of innocence, curiosity, and adventure—the ability to have fun no matter what. It's the look of love between good friends. It's childhood, every day reborn.

One thing is certain—I'll be going camping again.

Sales, Pails, and Car Pools

One of the great ironies of life is that kids count the days till school's *out* and parents count the days till school's *in*.

Summer vacation starts out like a picnic in the park and ends up like a life sentence in a Siberian work camp.

In the beginning of the summer, things flow smoothly. The children seem satisfied with swimming, baseball, ice cream, and reruns. By summer's end the kids wouldn't be happy if they owned Disneyland, Sea World, and the Rockies.

Getting your child ready for the school year requires a Ph.D. in fashion design, with undergraduate studies in stationery supply. A master's in lunch pails is also helpful.

When I announced that we were going shopping in order to prepare for the new school year, the kids cheered as if it were Christmas. To me it was Labor Day.

School clothes were first on the list. As we approached the racks I found myself gravitating to the bargains, while my children were drawn to the top-dollar designer labels.

"Here's a real steal of a deal!" I shouted from one end of the store.

"Look at this super French stuff," yelled the kids from the other side of the store.

"These clothes are French?" I muttered, looking down at the label bearing the name Jacques Schlock.

Well I learned quickly that if you want your children to be socially acceptable, you don't send them off to school in bargain brands. They'd rather go to school in a refrigerator carton. (I gave that serious consideration.)

Next it was on to the local stationery store for notebooks, paper, pencils, and pens. When I was a kid, notebook choosing was simple . . . blue or black. Now it's an exercise in advanced decision making. I watched my kids decide among:

- 37 colors (14 are fluorescent for carrying with you on a bike at night)
- 2-ring, 3-ring, 5-ring, 7-ring, or 12-ring
- options like pockets, file folders, writing boards, address books, calendars, clipboards, or wheels for skateboard conversions.

It took them longer to pick out a notebook than it took me to buy a new car!

Paper, pencils, and pens were chosen quickly in comparison. But then came the killer—lunch pails.

When I was young the only decision regarding lunch containers was whether or not you wanted your name on your brown bag.

Now I found myself looking over a sea of lunch pails representing every major football team, TV series, hit movie, successful novel, and comic strip character.

"Here's a nice one," I said pointing to a lunch pail with a local football team's emblem.

"No thanks," responded my son. "They'll have a bad season due to their lack of first-round draft picks."

"Oh," I mumbled. "How about this one?" I pointed to a pail with the star of a cute little television show.

"No good. They'll be canceled this season. Their Nielsen ratings are consistently low."

"Well, which one do you want?"

They went right for the team that would later win the World Series and the little movie character who would sweep the Oscars.

That night I sat down with my ledger to figure out the budget. By the time I paid off the "get ready for school" expenses, it would be Christmas.

I leaned back in my chair and thought about how complicated the world has become. Even the age-old rite of sending the kids off to school has been bombarded with the intricacies of unending choices. But I guess it's really not that new. My parents probably said the same of my generation, as did their parents before them.

I closed my ledger and got ready for bed. "Well, some things never change," I said to myself as I slipped into my Mickey Mouse Club pajamas with the pictures of Annette and Cubby on the shirt. "Kids will be kids."

With our shopping out of the way, the fateful day soon arrived. Rhonda was up early packing the lunch pails full of goodies. Remember the days of a peanut butter sandwich and a piece of fruit? Rhonda's in the kitchen preparing submarine sandwiches, ambrosia, prewrapped gourmet cheeses and crackers, German butterscotch pudding in tupperware, and a token of the bygone era— an apple.

"Don't worry," Joy whispered to Jesse. "You can trade that apple for some junk food once you get to the school cafeteria."

"Who would trade good junk food for an old apple?"

"Tommy will," she replied. "He has a horse."

"Hurry up you guys," Rhonda prodded. "Daddy's gonna drive you to school today, and we don't want to be late for the first day."

I glanced at my watch. "Relax, we've got plenty of time. The school's only six blocks away."

"Yes, but you're forgetting one thing, Dear."

I know when Rhonda calls me Dear it's a red alert.

"What am I forgetting, *Sweetums?*" I replied with the sincerity of a door-to-door salesman.

"We're in a car pool, My Love."

In that brief moment I realized that living six blocks from the school was a peripheral issue.

"Who else do I have to pick up?"

"Shannon, Amy, Kimmy, Lori, Eric, and Scott."

"Good grief, we should have left last night!" I sighed in exasperation.

"Most of them live close by, Honey. Relax."

"Wait a minute, wait a minute. What do you mean '*MOST* of them live close by'?"

"Well, Kimmy lives down in the next town."

"THE NEXT TOWN!!!"

"Calm down, Dear, your veins are showing."

"WHY DOES SHE GO TO THIS SCHOOL IF SHE LIVES IN THE NEXT TOWN?"

"She's a special student, Sweetie."

"Oh, that's just great," I fumed. "So I gotta burn all our good gas to go all the way to the next town to get a student who's special."

"Please, Honey, relax," Rhonda soothed. "You make the next town sound like Buenos Aires . . . by the way . . . speaking of burning good gas, the gas gauge is on *E*. You may want to stop and fill it up before you go too far."

"I may just run out of gas on purpose and make all those little devils push me to the school."

"That's fine, Dear," Rhonda replied. "Just remember they're all wearing new clothes. Try to keep them clean."

I loaded Joy and Jess into the car and started my whirlwind tour of our state.

Sometimes I'm just plain stupid. I should have gotten gas, gone to the next town to pick up Kimmy, and then grabbed the other five on the way back.

Instead, I picked up Amy, Eric, Lori, Scott, and Shannon right away.

So I pulled up to the gas station with seven kids hanging out of every available window, door, or rust hole in our station wagon.

I pulled over by the self-serve pump, figuring the time outside the car would be helpful in gaining perspective.

I unscrewed the gas cap, lifted the hose off the pump, and put the nozzle in the gas tank.

The next ten minutes were spent trying to get the little hook on the nozzle to work so that I wouldn't have to squeeze the handle.

I finally got it to work.

Just as the tank filled.

Suddenly I was swimming in the Great Gas Sea.

I fought frantically to turn the pump off. There was no cooperation. Apparently I had placed the hook against the handle in such a way that it created a permanent weld.

I was ultimately rescued by the attendant. However, his rescue did not come quickly. At least another six dollars of gas had flowed through town before he made his way over to my personal oasis.

After paying the attendant a week's worth of wages, I hopped into the car to head off for Kimmy's. The seven kids greeted me royally.

"OH, GROSS . . . HE SMELLS LIKE GAS!! IT'S SO BAD . . . WE'RE GONNA FIXIATE!"

So here I was, driving through town, with seven little heads hanging out the window, fervently gasping for clean air.

Scott poked Joy, "Tell your dad he left his gas cap at the gas station."

Joy refused, mumbling something to Scott about the value of life.

By the time we arrived at Kimmy's house I realized that it was going to take TWA to get those kids to school on time.

To further complicate matters Kimmy was "running a little late" (in the words of her mother).

I learned that day that when a mother comes out and says her kid is "running a little late" it really means she just woke up.

Now there were eight kids in the car (one with breakfast). And we were off again.

What do you see in your community when you're in your car and running late?

Here's what I saw:

- Every traffic light was red.
- Stop signs were multiplying like crazy.
- The entire police force was assembled on my route to school. This included the town's police, the county's sheriffs, the state police, and the National Guard.
- The new crossing guards didn't have their act totally together so we had to watch a little slow-motion crossing.
- Three separate fender benders.
- A funeral motorcade.
- Six detours.
- Four overheated engines.

Top it all off with eight separate restroom stops and it's a wonder we made it in time for their college graduation.

I pulled into the school parking lot and immediately noticed that I was the only man there. It was a little scary . . . me and 700 women and children. (I wonder . . . did King Solomon ever have days like this?)

Fortunately I only small-talked with a few people. Word spread quickly that the token male over in the station wagon was wearing "eau de gasoline."

As the car emptied out, the six little friends went their merry way with a halfhearted thank you and a quick little wave of the hand. Then, my own two precious little people got out, paused, came over to the window, reached in, gave me a big hug (gas and all), kissed me, and said, "We love you, Daddy."

They walked off to their new year of adventure, leaving Dad with the full spectrum of emotions.

Sales, Pails,
and Car Pools

I was happy to see them start a new year of challenge. I was fearful of people or circumstances that would shatter their little lives, knowingly or unknowingly. I was relieved that we had survived another summer vacation. I was hopeful that a routine would once again return to our home.

But most of all, I was sad. Our summer had been a great time together. Sure, there were times when the kids got bored, got antsy, and got on our nerves. But that time was so precious . . . irreplaceable. I was sorry that the time had gone by so quickly.

I couldn't believe it, but I found myself thinking, *I'm glad I have next summer to look forward to!* Me, a parent who'd been counting the days till school would be in, already longing for the next summer vacation!

A car pool sure can have a strange effect on a fellow!

Animal Crackers

What thoughts enter your mind when I say the words *Southern California?* Do you think of it as quiet, peaceful, conservative, status quo, and humdrum?

No, you probably think of it as the Land of Fruits, Nuts, and Granola.

Our family is just nutty enough to fit in quite well.

Yet, I can still recall a family outing that made me feel as though all of Southern California was a great big Saturday morning cartoon. It occurred in the strangest place—a pediatrician's office.

This particular children's doctor came highly recommended. He was known for his special appeal to the kids. He ran a clinic that he called "child-centered." I was soon to find out that he took all this "child-centered" stuff to the ultimate in Southern Californian expression.

When Rhonda came home with the first pediatrician's bill, I decided we'd all go together as a family. That way I could fire questions about all manner of human illness all in the name of one sick kid.

That's how a pediatrician's appointment became a family outing. We've gone as a group ever since.

Here's our visit to a pediatrician who had turned his office into Lion Country Safari:

We got up very early in the morning the day of the appointment. Our goal was to be the first ones in the office. That way we were only behind those who had camped out overnight.

As we drove up to the parking lot, there was a mechanical guardrail that lifted as you took a parking ticket. I am not unfamiliar with these devices. Yet this one was distinctively different.

It was painted up to look like a giraffe.

"Hi, this is JoJo the Giraffe," the ticket machine told me. "Just grab one of my tick-ticks and I will raise my neck so you can parky park!"

"Tick-tick? Parky park?" I groaned loud enough for all to hear. As I grabbed the ticket, JoJo continued.

"That's the way, boys and girls. Just drive right in and parky park 'cause now it's all righty-rooney."

"Gimmicks," I grumbled. "Even doctors resort to gimmicks."

"There's a cute one," Rhonda said as she pointed to a sign by the entrance. It said, See Sally Tate. She Valley Dates your tick-ticks. It was signed by JoJo Giraffe.

Rhonda leaned over and whispered in my ear. "During lunch hour, Sally Tate is a boy. All the nurses go to lunch, and they leave this poor little guy to do the validations. It's so embarrassing."

As I opened the door and walked in, there was no doubt that a pediatrician lived here. The decor was your basic Barnum and Bailey. Everything was balloons, clowns, smiling animals, and lollipops.

Out of the corner of my eye I noticed one of the smiling animals was moving. She was a nurse!

"Good morning, good morning! I'm Darla the Dancing Bear. Do you want to see the circus today?"

"No, we're here for his checkup," I said, pointing to the baby.

Darla frowned at me and cleared her throat. "That's what I mean, Sir."

"Oh . . . gee . . . I'm sorry . . . I didn't catch all the lingo at first. . . . Uh . . . yes . . . we want to see the circus."

"Fine," Darla replied. "Do you want to see Dr. Lion, Dr. Tiger, Dr. Zebra, or Dr. Chimp?"

By then I was totally bewildered. Fortunately, Rhonda had been through this before and calmly replied. "Dr. Lion, please."

"That's neato-mosquito," gushed Darla. "Go right over to the Red Balloon Room and I'll call for you when Dr. Lion is ready."

As we approached the Red Balloon Room, I noticed that they at least let the adults in on the color coding:

Red Balloon Room	**Well Children**
Blue Balloon Room	**Sick Children**
Green Balloon Room	***Really* Sick Children**

When we entered the Red Balloon Room, Rhonda immediately explained to me. "This is supposed to recreate the feeling inside the mother's womb."

The entire room was made to look like a giant red balloon. There were soft sounds of gentle, lapping water. The lights were low.

"Check your belly buttons, kids," I announced. "You'll be growing an umbilical cord any minute now."

"Hush, Bill," Rhonda whispered. "This is supposed to produce a calming psychological effect on the children."

"Okay," I said. But I couldn't resist one more jab. "I thought it was like this because it seems like you wait nine months to see the doctor."

I laughed out loud.

But I laughed alone.

Everyone else in the Red Balloon Room just stared at me in disgusted disbelief.

As I quickly glanced around the womb, it was abundantly clear that I was the token male adult. The only other males were less than three feet in height, complete with runny nose. Most were thumb suckers.

I also noticed that all the adult females had little crying children nestled in their arms. They were softly singing to them and gently rocking them from side to side in their arms. All the women seemed to be in cadence.

I started to feel seasick.

I was about to climb overboard when the piercing sound of a drumroll intervened.

"Attention all boys and girls," screamed a voice over the drumroll. "This is Connie the Cockatoo announcing that it is John Butterworth's turn to visit the circus."

This was followed by canned laughter and applause. I felt like I was in an old "I Love Lucy" rerun.

As we all walked out of the Red Balloon Room Womb, I whispered to Rhonda, "Well, Babe, this is what it's like to be born ... we're leaving the womb together ... think of it, Babe ... sextuplets!"

"That's all men think about," sighed a woman by the door. Rhonda's face matched the room color.

We followed Connie the Cockatoo to a door with a big sign that said, The Lion's Den.

"Is everybody ready to see the lion in the circus?" Connie was as excited as a game show host.

All the kids screamed in unison, "YEAH, MAN!"

"Well, heeeeeeere we go into the Lion's Den!"

She opened the door to reveal the most fascinating Lion's Den ever seen by human eyes.

It was an undercover examination room.

There was a padded examination table, sink, cabinets, shelves filled with cotton balls, tongue depressors, bandages, and stethoscopes. But there was one big difference: Everything had fur.

The table was furry, the sink was bordered with fur, the spigots were furry, the cabinets, shelves, and containers all looked like souvenirs from Lion Country Safari.

Connie the Cockatoo continued her canned corn. "Okay, Mom and Dad, put little Johnny-pooh on the table. Take off all his clothesey-wooseys including his dipe-wipe. Dr. Lion will enter his den reeeeeeeel soon."

This is always one of the more explosive times in the session. Any parent with young children knows you don't take the "dipe-wipe" off for more than three seconds at a time without living to regret it.

"I forgot my umbrella," I grumbled as I undressed John.

Rhonda was busy trying to keep the other kids out of trouble. It looked like they were into everything with fur. She was frantically trying to pick up tongue depressors while Jesse climbed up to the top fur shelf for his biggest move.

"Look, everyone ... it's snowing!" he yelled as he freely tossed cotton balls all over the Lion's Den.

The pressure was incredible.

I felt like Daniel.

Outside we heard the "GROOOWLLLL" of the approaching Dr. Lion. We frantically began picking up the snow, using the tongue depressors as shovels.

The door opened.

"G R R R R O O O W W W L L L L"

I couldn't believe my eyes.

Dr. Lion looked just like Bert Lahr in *The Wizard of Oz.*

I looked behind him for Dorothy and Toto, too.

"G R R R R O O O W W W L L L L!! I am friendly Dr. Lion. I love little boys and girls. Where is little Johnny Bonbon Butterworth?"

"There he is, Doc," volunteered Jesse, pointing to the exam table. "Go get him, Doc ... ZAP him!"

Dr. Lion smiled and broke into an indescribable laugh, "Ha, Ha, Ho, Ho, He, He, Hu, Hu, Yuk, Yuk, Yah, Yah, Ooh, Ooh, Ahh, Ahh, GROWL!"

Rhonda and I were staring in disbelief. The kids all started to imitate him.

It was a funny farm.

I don't remember the Cowardly Lion in the *Wizard of Oz* having pockets, but Dr. Lion had them. He reached into one and pulled out a variety of instruments to use for John's checkup.

"Okay, Mom and Dad, let's remove the dipe-wipe and take a look at this young cub."

Just as he reached over to pick up John, Dr. Lion suddenly fell back, almost to the furry floor. We looked behind him and saw the problem.

Jeffrey was pulling his tail.

Animal Crackers

"JEFFREY, NO!" Rhonda and I both yelled.

"It's okay, folks," soothed Dr. Lion. "It happens all the time." He turned to Jeffrey. "Here, Little Guy, wanna play with a scalpel?"

Rhonda paled.

"Just kidding, just kidding," chided Dr. Lion. He then burst into his widely imitated laugh, this time joined by all the kids. "Ha, Ha, Ho, Ho, He, He, Hu, Hu, Yuk, Yuk, Yah, Yah, Ooh, Ooh, Ahh, Ahh, GROWL!!"

The kids were having the time of their lives. I was thinking of taking my life.

The doctor checked John over and kept muttering positive sounds. "Uh-huh ... that's good ... Yes ... Very nice ... Fine ... Excellent ... Oh, my, wonderful ... Yeah, man ... Very good ... Neat ... Outstanding ... Cool, very cool ..."

Then he took a step back, looked at all the kids and said, "Well, well, well, how well do you think Baby John Bonbon is today?"

That must have been the cue, 'cause all at once all the kids and the human lion lifted their faces to the sky like howling coyotes and offered this medical diagnosis:

"HE'S GRRRRRRREAT!!"

"I thought it was a tiger that did that on television?" I quizzed.

"Yes, well, I think I borrowed that from Dr. Tiger," explained Dr. Lion, not the least bit ruffled. "As animal doctors, we need to be friends."

The kids were beaming from ear to ear, as if they had just learned words to live by.

"Now let's see," continued Dr. Lion, as he perused a furry clipboard. "Johnny-pooh is due today for his animal crackers for measles, mumps, and rubella."

"That means a needle, Dad," translated Joy.

"Can I have a rumbrella?" asked Jeffrey.

"Rubella, sweetie, rubella. It's a disease," Rhonda corrected.

"Oh," mused Jeffrey. "I don't want any shot that gives me diseases."

Rhonda and I looked at one another with our "What's the use?" expression.

Dr. Lion interrupted, "All right. I'll have Kathy Kangaroo hop over to the Lion's Den here and give some animal crackers to Baby John Bonbon."

"It sure has been fun, boys and girls," Dr. Lion went into his standard farewell. "You're just the best boys and girls I've ever seen." The kids were beaming from ear to ear. "You're great ... and I'm not *lyin'*."

I felt nauseous after that last sickening pun.

"Let's do the Dr. Lion Good-bye Growl. Ready? One, two, three ...."

"G R R R R O O O W W W L L L L"

It was an earshattering climax.

As Dr. Lion exited slowly, he reminded Rhonda, "Kathy Kangaroo will be here in a minute for the animal crackers."

Then he turned to me. He made no effort to continue his little lion act. He turned very adult, removed some paper from his furry clipboard and uttered three manly words: "Here's your bill."

With that, he was gone.

We tried our best to keep relative peace in the Lion's Den. Fortunately, it was not too long before we heard BOING, BOING, BOING, hopping down the hall toward us.

"Well, hello, boys and girls," she began. "I'm Kathy Kangaroo and I have some animal crackers for someone special!"

"I'm not special," blurted out Joy.

"Me neither," added Jesse.

"No rumbrella for me," said Jeffrey, still hopelessly confused.

"Well, where is Johnny Sweetums Butterworth?"

Five petrified people pointed to the defenseless victim.

"All right, let me see what's in my Kangaroo pouch for Baby John-John Honeypie."

The kids knew exactly what was going to happen. Kathy Kangaroo feeds you some animal crackers in order to get you to think about the top, while she prepares to send a sharp message to your bottom.

Sure enough, the same process unfolded and John ate the most painful meal known to man.

The needle sent John into a frenzy. He spit out the crackers, writhed, kicked, jumped, bit, punched, scratched, pulled hair, and worst of all . . . he wet.

"Here's his dipe-wipe," I offered Kathy Kangaroo, just a little too late.

"It's okay," she sighed, wiping herself dry. "It happens all the time."

We hurriedly dressed John and made our way out of the Lion's Den. We headed back to the front where Darla the Dancing Bear was waiting for payment in full.

Darla grabbed the bill with her right paw and began to calculate the total on an adding machine with her left paw.

"Let's see. Healthy baby checkup . . . measles, mumps, rubella shot . . . one box of tongue depressors . . . one jar of cotton balls . . . animal crackers . . . oh, yes, one last item . . . dry cleaning the kangaroo suit.

"Here's the total." She would not say it aloud so as to not disturb other patients. Instead she wrote the total down on a small piece of paper. Not too small, though, for it was a pretty large number.

"WOW!" I swallowed. "All that for a checkup? If they ever got sick, I'd go bankrupt."

"You can file next door in the lawyer's office if you'd like," said Darla straight-faced. "We have an excellent working relationship with them."

After I paid, we saw Sally Tate to "valley date" and we walked to the car. As we walked I overheard Joy and Jesse.

"You know why I like Dr. Lion, Jesse? 'Cause most places we go don't let kids have fun and it's all for big people. But when we go to see Dr. Lion, big people have to sit and be quiet and us kids can be exactly like we want."

"Yeah," replied Jesse. "Even when he growls, it's all for fun."

I thought to myself, *Gee I guess it is unusual for an adult to come down to a child's level. It's a shame adults like that are so rare.*

As we entered the car, I couldn't resist applying what I had just learned. "Hey, boys and girls, what do you think of Dr. Lion?"

Six loud voices replied at the top of their lungs.

"He's G R R R R R R R R R E E E E E E E E E A T!!! G R R R R O O O O W W W L L L L L!"

That day was a real value and encouragement to me.

You might call it a real animal cracker in the arm.

10

The Annual Elementary School Open House
and Musical Endurance Festival

Don't you just love autumn? I do.

Don't you just love colored leaves, football games, cooler weather, bowls of chili, fall fashions, pumpkins, and sending the kids off to school? I do.

However, there is one annual autumn event that I could gladly overlook ... maybe you know what I'm talking about.

At our house we call it the Annual Elementary School Open House and Musical Endurance Festival. You know, that special night when the parents go back to school.

Here's what happened at our last Festival:

When I arrived home from work on that fateful evening, Rhonda had my blue suit out on the bed. "We want to make a good impression on Joy and Jesse's teachers."

"What difference does it make?" I questioned. "The kids tell the teachers what we are *really* like anyway!"

"All the more reason to look nice and proper," replied Rhonda.

"Great," I mocked. "That way the teachers will be convinced that our kids are pathological liars."

Rhonda gave me her "You're gonna wear this blue suit even if it kills you" look and I submissively conceded.

Rhonda showed the baby-sitter where to find phone numbers for police, fire department, paramedics, lawyers, bail bondsmen, and the Marines. She then systematically kissed each child good-bye and they each "wiped it off" as soon as it was planted. I grabbed Rhonda's arm and scurried her out the front door. Being a gentleman, I opened her car door, seated her, closed her door, and hurried over to the driver's side. As I sat down and closed the door, I suddenly realized that this was not the neat little compact car I drive to and from work, it was the car that transports the kids.

I was sitting on a previously owned lollipop.

"Oh, no!" I lamented. "A sticky lollipop all over the seat of my blue suit pants!"

"Well, at least it was grape," consoled Rhonda. "The purple kinda blends in."

Her comforting fell on deaf ears. "Why is it that I always get stuff on me *ONLY* when I'm dressed up?" By then I was fuming.

"Calm down, Dear. We'll be at the school in a few minutes. I don't want you around other people while you're so angry."

"I may not be around anyone. I may be stuck to this seat indefinitely."

"Don't overreact, Dear. It's only a lollipop. It's not as bad as your famous Sunday Morning Paste Waffles." Rhonda laughed.

But she laughed alone.

Six blocks later we pulled up at the school. The parking lot was full of wives delivering last-minute lectures to their husbands. All the men looked like they were preparing to attend a workshop on "Your Future in Needlepoint." I saw guys who rarely wear shirts dressed in coats and ties. We were surrounded by men making the ultimate sacrifice for their children: They had buttoned the top button on their shirts.

We walked into the auditorium and our ears were greeted by the destructive sounds of the elementary band tuning up.

A few guys were applauding, obviously confusing tuning up with the actual concert. They *are* remarkably similar.

The principal stepped up to the platform and officially began the program by welcoming us. He then introduced the band, using glowing terms that tickled the ears of every band member and each accompanying set of parents.

The rest of us were sick.

The band broke into this year's version of "America the Beautiful." This year they are heavy on reeds and percussion, so there were plenty of squeaks and rhythms that defy description.

The mothers were bravely hanging in there, as dads quickly and quietly slipped from their seats to escape this POW-like atmosphere.

I started to get up, but Rhonda gave me a look that

said, "Stay," and anyway the seat of my pants was stuck to the auditorium chair.

The bandleader ended the piece, and it was not too long before all the band members did the same. Ending together has always been tough.

Next, it was "Stars and Stripes Forever." It was so effectively disguised that it could have faked out John Philip Sousa himself.

An observant dad in the front row began to pass back the explanation for the hideous sound:

The clarinet section was still playing "America the Beautiful."

This patriotic medley was soon bringing grown men to tears in emotion-filled love for their country.

The guy next to me leaned over and whispered, "Can you believe we're missing a special Thursday night edition of "Monday Night Football" in order to hear this impersonation of fingernails on a chalkboard?"

I was stunned.

I was willing to give up a normal evening to visit the local asylum ... but not the night of a football game.

"Who's playing?" I whispered.

"Miami and San Diego," he replied. "When I left it was 21–21 in the second quarter. It's a real aerial exhibition."

My thoughts of a wide receiver snatching up a bomb were hastily interrupted when the bass drum stand collapsed and sent the bass drum rolling toward the flutes.

Fortunately a trombone player stopped the drum before it crushed the petite little flute players. Most of the band had stopped playing, except for a few faithful clarinetists who obviously wanted to finish "America the Beautiful" before the Tricentennial.

Order was hastily regained and it was time for the band's last number: "The Battle Hymn of the Republic." It sounded so bad, I kinda wished the South had won the Civil War, 'cause I think this band could have done a better job with "Dixie."

A piece of paper was making its way around the men. It said, "Miami 31, San Diego 28 halftime."

Apparently one of the sound technicians in the back had his headphones plugged into the play-by-play of the game.

Lucky guy. It sure beat listening to "The Battle Hymn."

Not all the men were able to see the note. That's because many of the men who had kids in the band had the pleasant and relaxing task of taking pictures of this precious event.

Nobody just takes pictures anymore. These poor chumps were over on the side with tripods, audio microphone units, video recorders, light meters, floodlights, telephoto lenses that looked like telescopes, and instruction manuals that looked like Chicago phone books.

The band was really into "The Battle Hymn" by now, and I noticed that one of the dads was swearing because his audio microphone unit had just blown. Apparently it was not designed to record sounds of that intensity. It could only handle softer sounds like a blast-off of the space shuttle.

The frazzled bandleader was facing the audience, asking us to stand and join the band by singing the last chorus of this classic. This was tougher than it sounds because no one was really certain when or where to begin.

However, everyone gave it the old college try. It ended up being a predominantly female chorus as the men were once again circulating a note. "San Diego 34, Miami 31 on a 86-yard touchdown run. Extra point was blocked."

Things started to wind down. The few men that were singing finished up, followed by the women finishing four bars later. Eventually the band concluded in the following order: trumpets, saxophones, trombones, drums, flutes, and last, clarinets.

The applause was deafening. The adults were going wild over the fact that this portion of the program was OVER.

During the transition, the principal was sharing extemporaneous remarks. No one could hear him though, because all the band members were packing up their instruments and the photo-finish fathers were packing up thousands of dollars' worth of camera equipment.

As the noise level began to soften, we faintly heard about coffee and cookies in the cafeteria, followed by the open house in your child's classroom.

The thought of food caused the men to hustle. It started to look like the Raiders' locker room as grown men began pushing and shoving in order to obtain a Lorna Doone.

I was right in there in the thick of it.

Rhonda and all the other women were standing back, shaking their heads and clucking their tongues in disgust.

They were just jealous.

Unfortunately, as I reached for a Fig Newton, I was struck with the judgment of God.

The guy next to me spilled his coffee all over the front of my blue suit.

So there was grape lollipop on the seat of my pants, Maxwell House on the front of my jacket, and a consoling wife on my arm.

She was laughing her head off.

We started to make our way to Joy's classroom when I got another note pushed into my paw: "34–34 Tie, early in fourth quarter."

This was torture at its finest. The NFL was delivering the finest competition of the season, and I was stuck in an elementary school wearing lollipops and coffee.

Truly sadistic.

We found Joy's room and entered. It had been so long since I'd been in a classroom (a full year) I had forgotten how small everything looked. This was emphasized by the sight of grown adults attempting to sit at their children's desks.

Rhonda sat down at Joy's desk, and I sat nearby at a desk without a name.

"That's where we seat the children who misbehave," announced the teacher, pointing at me.

Forty-five adults turned and coldly stared at me with steely eyes.

"You'd be surprised what goes on at that desk," the teacher giggled.

I was not the slightest bit amused.

I decided I was going to slide the chair out from under the desk and move it away from the spotlight. Yet, as I removed my left leg from under the desk I was met with the surprise of my life—bubble gum.

You've got it folks. Bright pink, already-been-chewed bubble gum spread all over the left thigh of a once clean blue suit.

By now the teacher was passionately involved in explaining workbooks and readers. My attention span had expired however. I sat there examining my latest malady—pink thigh.

Like any person who is bored, I started to fool around

with anything I could find. I started scribbling with pencils, pens, and crayons. Just nice, safe, innocent doodling.

Among the pens, however, was one that was apparently out of ink. I scribbled and scribbled and scribbled, but the pen refused to cooperate.

This fired my manly juices. I decided I was going to get this pen to work before the teacher got on to her next point: "You and Your Child's Lunch Pail."

So I pulled the pen apart and began to examine the ink cartridge. I did all the manly things I should. I shook it, hit it, blew into it, bent it—the whole bit.

Shaking, hitting, and blowing were fine.

Bending was a real mistake.

It snapped in two.

I found the missing ink.

It splotched onto my coat sleeve, shoulder, and right lapel.

It looked terrible. Especially with pink thigh.

I did the only manly thing I could think of. I put my head down on my desk and began sobbing uncontrollably.

When I regained my composure and raised my head, I discovered I had ink on my cheek and forehead.

Meanwhile a new note was circulating: "Still 34–34, two-minute warning."

By now I was sick to my stomach. This was not a man's ultimate fantasy. Somehow sitting at a first grader's desk while in a blue suit that is sticky, inky, gummy, creamy, and sugary is less than masculine.

It also smells terrible.

Fortunately, the teacher was concluding her remarks on her final topic: "The Educational Value of Recess."

She closed by saying, "Now, before you leave, please

The Annual
Elementary School
Open House
and Musical Endurance Festival

make sure that we meet one another personally. I'd hate for your son or daughter to be educationally disadvantaged because we were unable to chat for a few minutes."

The line formed quickly to meet the teacher. The plan was a quick handshake, smile, and speedy exit. Of course, everyone had that plan, so by the time I de-stuck myself from the desk, chair, paper, and a variety of other school supplies, we were the literal end of the line.

To make matters worse, whomever was our source for the football game must have been at the head of the line, for no one could update the score past the two-minute warning.

Well, it was one of those lines where a twenty-minute wait seemed like the Seven-Year Tribulation Period. I was in agony over having to wait so long. Everyone else was in agony over being near the smell of Candy-Coffee-Ink Man.

It was finally our turn.

"Hello, I'm Mrs. Burns."

"Hi," Rhonda replied. "We're Joy's mom and dad, Rhonda and Bill Butterworth."

Mrs. Burns shook Rhonda's hand politely, then turned to me and attempted to remain calm.

Rhonda tried to soften the blow. "He doesn't always look like this," she said.

"That's right," I added. "I seldom wear this suit, except for special occasions."

"Well . . . uhhh . . . let's see . . ." Mrs. Burns was stumbling. ". . . I certainly see now where Joy gets her creativity!"

We all laughed politely.

Mrs. Burns turned to Rhonda and continued, "Joy is a fine little student. She's never a behavior problem and it's simply a delight to work with her."

The fluff went on for a few more minutes. Then we all shook hands, which enabled me to transfer blue ink to the teacher. We left the room.

"Oh, my," Rhonda sighed, staring at the clock in the hall, "we spent so much time in there, we won't even be able to visit Jesse's room tonight."

"Boy, is that ever a disappointment," I mocked.

I ran to the car, cranked it up, turned on the radio, and tuned to every station. Not one would state the outcome of the football game.

We drove the six blocks home in silence.

There's not much to say when you're in your best blue suit with lollipop on the seat, coffee on the jacket, bubble gum on the thigh, ink on the lapel and sleeve, and the proverbial egg on your face.

That says it all.

As I ended the evening with the "Eleven O'Clock News," our local sports reporter capped my frustration with his lead story:

"Sports fans are calling it the most exciting NFL football game in recent history. If you missed it in Miami tonight, you really missed it . . . ."

On the way to bed I counted four little heads and wondered, *Have I really missed it?* It all depends on what "it" is supposed to be. I could never be a linebacker for the Dolphins or kick field goals for the Chargers, but I can do my job as a dad.

And part of that job is the Annual Elementary School Open House and Musical Endurance Festival.

The NFL has nothing on us fathers. Maybe that's why half of all parents are fathers—so they can learn what it means to be real men.

Some Things
Never Change

Do certain aspects of your family life resist change? They do at our place.

It's kind of like the law of gravity—you know—"What goes up must come down." At our house, no matter how hard we try to straighten up, there are some things that always come down the same.

You know the types of things I'm talking about. Things like the washing machine will always eat one sock or no one will need the bathroom until you do or (even as I write these words) your two-year-old won't need you until you sit down to do something else.

Well, I have a Some-Things-Will-Never-Change List.

So, let me share with you some pertinent examples with the appropriate background material.

1. THE KIDS WILL ALWAYS BE IN FRONT OF THE TELEVISION DURING THE MOST IMPORTANT SCENE.

This will never change at our house. So rather than making a resolution to shoot BB's at their ankles, I've decided to accept this as an unchangeable law of nature.

It makes no difference what show is on. Children have an uncanny sense of timing. During a football game, they come to life at the two-minute warning. During a whodunit, they begin blockage precisely at the moment the culprit is identified. During sitcoms they keep from my view all sight gags.

2. THE PHONE WILL ALWAYS RING DURING DINNER.

I hear about all these guys who use their evening mealtime as quality time for building character and conviction and strong family relationships. I just laugh because our family eats together once every three years. A prime problem is the phone. It never fails; as soon as we sit down, we pray, pass the potatoes, and answer the phone.

Don't tell me to take the phone off the hook. I'm married to the kind of woman who goes tapioca over a move like that. We tried it once and she spent the entire meal muttering, "I wonder who's trying to call us now?" and "What if there is an emergency and someone needs to get in touch with us?"

3. MY TWO-YEAR-OLD WILL AL-WAYS COLOR ON THE PER-SONAL MAIL, NEVER THE JUNK MAIL.

Our mailbox is a refuge for runaway junk mail. We get it by the ton. Occasionally, very occasionally, we receive an authentic personal letter. Somehow Jeffrey can smell it out of a seven-inch stack of junk mail. He'll take it over to the crayon corner and do a real number on it. By the time I get home from work, I see a piece of personal mail that has become a palette for abandoned crayons.

So if you've ever written to me and gotten no response, I want you to know that it's nothing personal.

4. SCREWDRIVERS, SCISSORS, TAPE, AND PLIERS MUST WALK, FOR THEY ARE NEVER WHERE YOU LAST PUT THEM.

To get the full value of this statement, it is important to realize that when you look for these things you will be deeply involved in a project. It is in the very heat of construction that you require the pliers. After a quick look in the drawer where they usually reside, it is common to frantically search drawers, closets, cans, jars, refrigerators, stoves, microwaves, toilets, and tubs.

This pressure is further intensified by the realization that the pliers belong to your neighbor.

5. GIVEN OUR TWO CARS TO CHOOSE FROM, I WILL ALWAYS DRIVE OFF WITH THE ONE THAT NEEDS GAS.

I have a terrible memory when it comes to gas tanks. Since I gas up a car at least once a day, I get them mixed up.

If I didn't see our neighbors at the gas station occasionally, I'd be tempted to believe they are siphoning my gas tanks late at night.

6. KIDS WILL ALWAYS NEED DIAPER CHANGES AT THE ABSOLUTE WORST TIMES.

You can count on this one every time. It may be during the best play of the game, it may be when you're having special guests for dinner. It may be when you're out in the car, miles away from diapers ... and you have no spare. It may be late at night when you're enjoying a romantic smooch on the couch. It may be just as you arrive at church. Or as you sit down to eat breakfast. It can happen during a long-distance phone call that's costing you a day's pay. It may happen after you spend ninety minutes getting the lawn mower started ... only to find it necessary to turn it off. It will always occur when you visit other homes in which there are no children.

You pick the bad time and wait for that whiff of wonderment that brings grown men to their knees begging for mercy. It's an unpleasant sight, indeed.

7. WHEN YOU'RE ON THE TELE-PHONE, PENCIL AND PAPER WILL NEVER BE NEARBY.

I think the part that frustrates me the most about all this is the fact that right next to our phone stands an *empty* pencil holder and a piece of cardboard that once had a tablet attached to it.

There is a variation to this rule. If the pencil and paper *are* nearby, the pencil will be without a point and the paper will be covered front and back with doodling from a previous call.

8. THE DISHES ARE NEVER DONE.

A sobering reality of life. It's amazing to me that our kids can totally disregard cleanliness in certain aspects, but when it comes to getting a drink of water, it is essential that they use a clean glass each time.

If Joy decides to make peanut butter and jelly sandwiches for herself and the boys, she uses one knife for her peanut butter; another knife for her jelly, and a third knife to cut her sandwich in half. Then she starts all over again for each of the boys' sandwiches. She'll put each sandwich on a plate, plus each child gets another plate for chips and a third plate for fruit.

So lunchtime snacks translate into twelve knives, four glasses, and twelve dishes, not counting spills.

How can you have kids and not count spills?

9. YOU NEVER ORDER THE PROPER AMOUNT OF FOODS FOR KIDS AT A RESTAURANT.

All the way to the eating establishment you hear the grieving, agonizing groans brought on by starvation. So when you get to the restaurant you figure it's all right for each child to order his own meal. You don't mind buying four meals if you know they will all be consumed.

The kids who yelp the loudest fill up the fastest. Three or four bites into the meal they are "stuffed." You think about another type of stuffing, but quickly dispel the thought for reasons of personal conscience.

The other extreme is ordering light only to discover your kids have turned into the Houston Oilers. They are scarfing down everything in sight ... including your meal.

This is frustrating indeed as you go away hungry, yet paying for nineteen meals.

Well, that should give you a little bit of an idea on how I constructed my "Some Things Never Change List." Televisions, telephones, junk mail, scissors, tape, pencils, paper, dishes, and diapers are all things that will never change. They just go on and on.

But, you know, those little blond-haired imps I call my children are far from changeless. They are different every day. Sure, there are certain bad habits they get into, but all that is transitory when you look at the big picture.

For that mystical magic of *growth* comes to visit on a daily basis. As much as I wish I could freeze their little lives at this tender age, I cannot. They continue to press on to maturity and consistently amaze me in the process.

Yet, because I'm so deeply committed to those kids, I can enjoy every moment. I've surrounded myself with people who say to me, "Enjoy the children now, while they're young." That's good advice.

When the kids become teenagers, I have another group of friends I'll bring around me to say, "These teen years are the best years between parents and children." The second group is sadly smaller, but it does exist. I want to do my best to add to it.

Yes, "Take God seriously, but don't take yourself so seriously," is probably some of the best advice I've ever received. I hope that it becomes a motto for my life that will never change.

I would like our home to always be a house of:

laughter and love,
   acceptance and affirmation,
      prayer and passion,
         realism and rest,
            integrity and intimacy,
               holiness and hugs,
                  tears and trust,
                     good times and godliness.

Well, Jeffrey has been trying to get my attention all the while I've been finishing up these thoughts. It looks like he's a great example of one last unchangeable rule of nature:

**10. *WHEN A LITTLE BOY FRAN-
TICALLY DANCES FROM ONE
FOOT TO THE OTHER . . . IT'S
TOO LATE.***

Some Things
Never Change